D0344942

Vegetarian APPETIZERS

by Paulette Mitchell

PHOTOGRAPHS BY
VICTORIA PEARSON

CHRONICLE BOOKS
SAN FRANCISCO

ACKNOWLEDGMENTS The creation of this book depended on the talents, skills, and hard work of many special people. I'd like to thank Jane Dystel, my agent, for her sound advice; Bill LeBlond, my Chronicle editor, for making this idea a reality; Chronicle editorial assistant Amy Treadwell, who orchestrated the schedule; Jan Hughes for her attention to detail; Benjamin Shaykin, who created the appealing design; Victoria Pearson for her outstanding food photography; and Michelle Fuller for promoting this and my other Chronicle project.

Finally, I thank my friends Raghavan Iyer, Nathan Fong, Cynthia Myntti, Marcia Rogers, Mary Evans, Beth Dooley, Fran Lebahn, Chandra Masloski, Tom Nugent, Barb Kennedy, Nancy Cameron, and Linda Platt for their encouragement and love. And my gratitude to Darryl Trones and my son, Brett, who contributed to this project with hearty appetites, help with the dishes, and never ending support.

Thank you all for being enthusiastic about *Vegetarian Appetizers*.

Library of Congress Cataloging-in-Publication Data available.

ISBN 0-8118-2966-9
Printed in China.

Prop Stylist: Ann Johnstad
Food Stylist: Christine Masterson
Food Stylist Assistant: Owen Masterson
Photographer's Assistant: Jon Nakano

Book and Cover Design: Benjamin Shaykin
Typeset in Fournier, Saracen, and Scala Sans

Distributed in Canada by Raincoast Books
9050 Shaughnessy Street
Vancouver, BC V6P 6E5

10 9 8 7 6 5 4 3 2 1

Chronicle Books LLC
85 Second Street
San Francisco, California 94105

www.chroniclebooks.com

contents

introduction

I love a good party, especially my own. Parties—be they splashy bashes or casual gatherings—mark milestones in my life: the housewarming for my first home, a baby shower for my best friend, a feast to share recipes gathered abroad, a cookbook publication celebration, an unforgettable dinner for two.

These days, as a veteran party giver, cooking teacher, cookbook author, and mother of a teenage son, I find myself cutting back on formality and fuss. Rarely is there time for preparing multicourse extravaganzas. By offering an array of small plates and finger foods, I free up my time in the kitchen to spend with the guests. The lively combinations here are culled from my years traveling through the United States, France, Italy, Greece, Turkey, and the Mediterranean. They capture exotic flavors in the form of hors d'oeuvres and small bites.

LITTLE PLATES FOR BIG IMPACT

Are you headed to the theater? Dreaming of a candlelit dinner? Catching up with old friends passing through town? Hosting a holiday open house?

Little plates are ideal when time is an issue. They may be served quickly and elegantly, or stretched out at a leisurely pace. Whether served at a planned occasion or an impromptu gathering, they are less demanding than a multicourse meal with all the attending china and utensils.

The term *hors d'oeuvres* literally means "outside the work," dishes usually served and eaten away from the dining table. As the translation implies, they are liberating for both hostess and guest. They provide the cook flexibility and creativity in the kitchen and allow the party movement and flow. Guests can move through a buffet line or travel the lines of conversation. Most dishes can be made in advance, making serving and cleanup a snap.

The recipes here are divided into chapters based on the size and type of dish. "Light bites" are perfect before a sit-down dinner. You may create a full meal by offering an array of appetizers from several chapters, ending with "sweet bites." Pair one or two "mezzo bites" with a soup or salad for a light supper; serve a couple for an easy lunch. Use "sizable bites" as the foundation for an appetizer buffet or serve them as a side dish to a light entrée. Many appetizers travel well and are easy to eat, perfect for picnics and potlucks. Simply multiply quantities to serve a crowd. Or, prepare a few elegant, artistically presented dishes to serve as a romantic dinner for two.

These recipes are based on fresh vegetables, and all are meatless; many are suitable for vegans or may be made so. There's something for every occasion, whether fancy finger food for a formal cocktail party, or dips and salsas for a casual gathering in the garden. Some recipes can be prepared quickly from staples for unexpected guests. You'll find suggestions for advance preparation, plus tips for combining simple recipes to make more elaborate presentations. Some of the recipes have dozens of possible uses, so let them serve as inspiration for your own creativity.

TIP

If you double a recipe, do not double the amount of herbs or spices. Use just a little more than in the original recipe, then add more to taste.

PLAN TO PLAN

Whether you're sending out formal invitations or catching friends at the last minute by phone, make a plan. I start with four lists: a recipe list, a shopping list, a serving dish and utensil list, and a calendar with preparation tasks assigned to each day.

Remember: For a large party, there's little reward and not much fun in doing it all yourself. If you'd like, pair these recipes with a few gourmet items from a specialty market or deli (elegant cheeses, assorted nuts, imported olives). Think about hiring someone or enlisting a friend to help with last-minute preparation, serving, and cleanup. When the guests arrive, be a gracious host and enjoy your own party.

Don't put off what you can do in advance. Make the do-ahead dishes (or components) a few days before. Set up the tables and ready the room a day or two ahead.

Select recipes by keeping in mind your guest list, the tone of the party, the season, the time of day, the length of the event, and whether or not the party includes other food (will these appetizers by followed by dinner?). I usually stick to a single cuisine if, for example, the dishes are to be served preceding an Asian or Italian menu. If the appetizers are themselves the main event, I usually pick a medley of recipes representing a variety of cuisines. As a general rule, I always choose one spectacular appetizer that's sure to impress, no matter how many people or what else I'm serving.

If your guests are diet-conscious, remember that you can use low- or nonfat dairy products, such as sour cream, cream cheese, or yogurt. Use low-sodium soy sauce and cholesterol-free mayonnaise, if you wish, when preparing the recipes. Provide a few vegan choices for guests who many not eat eggs or dairy products.

If the appetizers precede dinner, I usually serve two or three recipes, allowing two to four portions per person per recipe. For these, I usually choose "light bites" to avoid overwhelming the appetite.

If you're serving a selection of appetizers as the main event, select an assortment of four to six different dishes. Assuming that most cocktail parties run for two to four hours, allow four "light bites" per guest for the first two hours; about three per guest after that. Or, plan two "mezzo bites" and one or two "sizable bites" per person. It's better to be safe and make a little more food than you think you'll need. (Most of the dishes make great leftovers.) Have extra crackers and cheese on hand just in case you run short.

MIX AND MATCH

Select recipes for variety and balance: hot with cold, creamy with crunchy, savory with sweet, light with substantial. For an attractive presentation, make sure the appetizers vary in color and shape. And choose from the categories of vegetables, fruits, cheeses, nuts, breads, and pastries.

Budget your time. Dips are quick and hold well in the refrigerator for several days (improving if the flavors have a chance to marry). Some recipes make large quantities (pizzas and frittatas) and can be made in a large pan, then cut into smaller portions. Choose only one or two appetizers requiring last-minute assembly. Allow yourself enough time to fuss over that one spectacular showstopper that requires individual artistic assembly.

SERVING IN STYLE

Decide whether you'll plate and pass the food or present it on tables. Buffets work well for serving lots of people over an extended period of time (an open house, for example). Be sure to check frequently to keep the platters full and fresh looking. For smaller groups, it's fun to mingle with your guests as you make the rounds with a tray of hot appetizers.

If the event will last for several hours, start with light and fresh nibbles and move into more substantial dishes, then, time permitting, move back to fresh and light. Keep the guests guessing. If it's an appetizer party, finish with a few "sweet bites," fresh fruit, flavored coffee, or mint tea as a simple finale and a signal that the party's almost over.

PRESENCE AND PRESENTATION

You'll be using fresh, top-notch ingredients, and the food will look beautiful, so keep the presentation simple and eclectic. Bring out the silver trays, if you wish. Or use glass, china, pottery, or wooden containers. Vary shapes, sizes, and textures with baskets, bowls, and platters. Line them with cabbage, kale, lemon, or paper leaves. Or, spread a platter with a layer of uncooked dried beans, such as black beans or split peas, peanuts, or rock salt to serve as a backdrop for the food.

One perfect blossom, a bouquet of fresh herbs, or a shiny lemon leaf is often all a tray needs. Position garnishes so that the dishes will remain attractive as the food is eaten (e.g., place a raffia-tied bunch of herbs in the corner). For color, lightly spray the rim of a plate with oil and dust it with turmeric or paprika. Use cookie cutters to cut hearts, stars, and rounds from slices of bread or tortillas. Make edible containers from endive or radicchio leaves, hollowed-out bell peppers, or cooked potatoes. Simple artistic touches will make a lasting impression.

Generally, arrange only one recipe per tray. This is aesthetically pleasing and practical. It's awkward to present guests with too many choices, especially when they are engaged in conversation.

Determine how you'd like the guests to move about the room. Do you want to set all the food on one table, or would several small tables ease congestion and flow? When setting up the buffet, place containers on different levels. Vary the height by using tiered trays, or place containers on napkin-covered upside-down boxes or bowls.

While many of the appetizers don't require utensils, plates are a must, even for finger food. Make sure you have plenty of napkins.

Allow at least four paper cocktail napkins per hour of food, and keep them within easy reach. (If you use cloth napkins, make sure they're small, not dinner-size.)

Use 4- to 6-inch bread-and-butter plates (china, glass, paper, or plastic). This allows guests to take more than one item at a time.

Make sure there are places to deposit the debris of a party: pits, toothpicks, plastic spears, used napkins, and plates.

VEGAN RECIPES

The recipes in this book are meatless, relying on fresh, seasonal vegetables. Many are vegan, or not made with animal-derived foods, including dairy products (butter, cheese, milk) and eggs. These recipes, for strict vegetarians who eat neither meat nor animal-derived foods, have been determined using the basic recipe without variations or suggested accompaniments. Each is marked "vegan recipe" following the yield line. Please note that some breads, tortillas, and pitas may contain milk or egg products, so it is suggested that you read the fine print on their ingredients labels. By eliminating dairy products, such as dairy-based sauces or cheese, some of the other recipes in the book can become vegan.

On page 141, you'll find a list of the vegan recipes in this book.

paulette's tips

APPETIZER BASICS

This chapter includes the basic components of an appetizer repertoire. You'll rely on Roasted Red Bell Peppers (page 21) and Guacamole (page 17) when you're in a crunch for time or in a pinch for what to serve. By themselves or as a component to a more elaborate dish, they always please. Here, too, you'll find recipes for edible containers and homemade chips, crostini, and crisps to add personality and interest to any appetizer tray.

basil pesto

MAKES ⅓ CUP (*vegan recipe*)

This fragrant paste is great spread on Crostini (page 24) or Toast Points (page 29). For a quick dip, stir about ¼ cup pesto into ½ cup plain yogurt, mayonnaise, or sour cream; sprinkle with Parmesan cheese and season to taste.

1 cup loosely packed fresh basil leaves (see Tips)
¼ cup pine nuts (see Tips)
2 tablespoons extra-virgin olive oil
2 cloves garlic, minced, or 1 teaspoon prepared minced garlic
¼ teaspoon freshly ground pepper
⅛ teaspoon salt, or to taste

process all the ingredients in a food processor (or blender) until the mixture is a coarse purée. Taste and adjust the seasoning.

---

tips To store fresh herbs, wrap the stem ends with a moist paper towel, put in a sealed plastic bag, and refrigerate. Or, place the bunch, stems down, in a glass of water and cover with a plastic bag, securing the bag to the glass with a rubber band; change the water every 2 days. The herbs will last for about 1 week (it's best to use them within a few days). Just before using, wash the herbs in cool water and dry with paper towels or in a salad spinner.

Pine nuts, also called *pignoli,* are the seeds from the cones of certain pine trees. Their natural oil turns rancid very quickly, so they should be refrigerated for no more than 1 month or frozen for up to 3 months in a tightly closed container.

VARIATION Roasted-Garlic Basil Pesto: Substitute 4 cloves Roasted Garlic (page 20) for the fresh garlic and add 1 teaspoon fresh lemon juice.

After puréeing the pesto, stir in about 2 tablespoons freshly grated Parmesan cheese. (Do not freeze with the added cheese.)

ADVANCE PREPARATION The pesto will keep for up to 1 week in a covered container in the refrigerator; pour a thin film of olive oil on top of the pesto to prevent discoloration. For longer storage, spoon the mixture into an aluminum foil–lined custard cup; cover tightly with foil and freeze. Once frozen, remove the foil-wrapped packet and store in a freezer bag for up to 2 months.

guacamole

MAKES ABOUT ½ CUP

Say "adios" to guacamole in plastic tubs. Here's the real thing. Use it as a layer when filling Toasted Tortilla Cups (page 30) or as a dip for Crispy Tortilla Triangles (page 27).

1 ripe avocado, peeled and quartered (see Tip)
1 tablespoon fresh lime or lemon juice
1 tablespoon finely chopped onion
2 teaspoons plain yogurt or sour cream
2 cloves garlic, minced, or 1 teaspoon prepared minced garlic
⅛ teaspoon Tabasco sauce, or to taste
⅛ teaspoon freshly ground pepper, or to taste
Salt to taste

process all the ingredients in a food processor (or blender) until smooth and creamy. Taste and adjust the seasoning.

refrigerate in a covered container for at least 1 hour before serving. Serve chilled or at room temperature.

tip The two most common varieties of avocados are the Fuerte, which has a smooth green skin, and the pebbly textured, almost-black, rich-flavored Haas, which I prefer. Select fruits that are unblemished and heavy for their size. Most avocados require a few days of ripening after purchasing; place them in a pierced paper bag at room temperature for a day or two to speed up the process. The avocados will yield to a gentle pressure when they are ripe and ready to use. Store ripe avocados in the refrigerator for up to 5 days. Once cut and exposed to the air, avocado flesh discolors rapidly; to minimize this, coat the cut surfaces with lime or lemon juice, and add these juices to recipes containing avocado.

ADVANCE PREPARATION The guacamole will keep for up to 2 days in a covered container in the refrigerator.

red pepper–corn salsa

MAKES 2⅓ CUPS *(vegan recipe)*

Serve this colorful, fresh salsa in a bowl for dipping Crispy Tortilla Triangles (page 27) or layer it with Guacamole (page 17) in Toasted Tortilla Cups (page 30).

2 tablespoons fresh lime or lemon juice (see Tips)
1 tablespoon extra-virgin olive oil
1 tablespoon minced jalapeño chile, or to taste
2 cloves garlic, minced, or 1 teaspoon prepared minced garlic
Salt and freshly ground pepper to taste
1 cup diced red bell pepper
1 cup frozen corn, thawed
2 green onions (white and green parts), coarsely chopped (about ⅓ cup)
2 tablespoons minced fresh cilantro or basil

stir together the lime or lemon juice, oil, jalapeño, garlic, salt, and pepper in a medium bowl. Add all the remaining ingredients; toss to mix. Taste and adjust the seasoning. Serve chilled or at room temperature.

tips Freshly squeezed citrus juice is always the most flavorful. Avoid the chemical-laden and artificial-tasting reconstituted lemon and lime juices that come in bottles and plastic "lemons" and "limes."

When selecting citrus fruits for juicing, the best are those that have a fine-textured skin and are heavy for their size. To squeeze more juice from citrus fruits, first bring them to room temperature, or microwave chilled fruit (pierce the fruit with a fork or knife first) for 30 seconds on high. Then roll the fruit around on a hard surface, pressing hard with the palm of your hand for a minute or so, to break the inner membranes.

VARIATION Substitute grilled sweet corn cut from the cob for the frozen corn.

ADVANCE PREPARATION The salsa will keep for up to 2 days in a covered container in the refrigerator.

roasted garlic

(*vegan recipe*)

Roasting gives garlic a buttery texture and a mild, sweet flavor (see Tips). Spread it on Crostini (page 24) just as it comes out of the oven or on the warm toast before topping it with tomatoes and basil when you make Tomato-Basil Bruschetta (page 88). You can use roasted garlic as an ingredient in most recipes calling for garlic, such as Basil Pesto (page 16), so roast several bulbs at a time and use liberally.

preheat the oven to 400°F. Line a baking sheet or small pan with aluminum foil.

for each whole garlic bulb, gently remove the loose, excess papery skin. Trim off the top stem, but leave the cloves intact. Lightly brush the skin and top with olive oil and place the bulb on the prepared pan. (Roast as many bulbs at one time as you'd like.)

bake for about 20 to 25 minutes, or until the garlic cloves feel very soft when pierced with the tip of a knife. Transfer to a plate to cool.

to use, separate the individual garlic cloves; slice the bottom from each and squeeze at the end to release the roasted garlic.

---

tips Select bulbs that are clean and firm to the touch. Store in a cool, dark, well-ventilated place such as a garlic cellar (a ceramic pot with holes and a lid); or seal in a plastic bag and refrigerate. Unbroken bulbs will keep for 2 months; individual cloves for 10 days. Sprouted cloves are usable, but less flavorful.

The more garlic is cooked, the milder it becomes. Roasting produces a mild, sweet, nutty flavor; boiling, a mild flavor; sautéing, a moderately strong flavor with more bite than boiled garlic, but with less intensity than raw garlic.

VARIATION To roast garlic in the microwave: Place the prepared garlic bulb on a paper towel. Microwave on high for 1 minute; turn the bulb upside-down, then microwave for about 1 minute more, or until soft.

ADVANCE PREPARATION Roasted garlic bulbs will keep for up to 3 days in plastic wrap or in a covered container in the refrigerator.

roasted red bell peppers

(vegan recipe)

A must in Roasted Red Pepper- and Feta-Stuffed Zucchini Cups (page 52), Roasted Red Pepper Hummus (page 43), and Roasted Red Bell Pepper Sauce (page 22), and so tasty that they're great on their own. These peppers take only 30 minutes and will keep in the refrigerator to use later.

preheat the broiler. Line a baking sheet with aluminum foil.

for each bell pepper, remove the stem and cut the pepper in half lengthwise; discard the seeds, membranes, and stem. Place the pepper halves, skin-side up, on the baking sheet; flatten each with the palm of your hand. (Place as many pepper halves as you'd like on the baking sheet, arranging them in a single layer.) Lightly brush the skins with olive oil.

broil for about 10 minutes, or until the peppers are fork-tender and the skins are blackened, charred, and blistered.

while they are still hot, transfer the peppers to a heavy-duty zip-top plastic bag and seal; set aside until cool, about 10 to 15 minutes. (The steam will loosen the skins.) Remove the peppers from the bag; peel and discard the skins.

tip Red bell peppers are vine-ripened green peppers and are sweeter because of the longer ripening. Choose peppers that are plump, firm, and crisp, with no wrinkling or soft spots. Store them for up to 1 week in plastic bags in the refrigerator.

VARIATION Roast bell peppers on a grill over a hot charcoal fire or over the open flame of a gas stove.

ADVANCE PREPARATION Roasted bell peppers will keep for up to 2 days in a covered container or plastic bag in the refrigerator. Drain well before using. Or, marinate the roasted and peeled bell peppers in extra-virgin olive oil and season with salt and pepper; refrigerate in a tightly closed jar.

roasted red bell pepper sauce

MAKES ABOUT ½ CUP *(vegan recipe)*

Taste the Mediterranean sunshine captured in this versatile sauce. Top Crostini (page 24), drizzle over Roasted Vegetable Antipasto (page 76), or use as a dip for Wontons with Herbed Tomato Sauce (page 100) and Savory Nut Balls (page 105).

½ cup chopped Roasted Red Bell Pepper (page 21), or jarred roasted red bell pepper, well drained
1 tablespoon extra-virgin olive oil (see Tip)
2 teaspoons fresh lemon juice
1 clove garlic, minced, or ½ teaspoon prepared minced garlic
1 teaspoon sugar
¼ teaspoon freshly ground pepper, or to taste
⅛ teaspoon salt, or to taste

process all the ingredients in a food processor (or blender) until smooth. Taste and adjust the seasoning.

tip Extra-virgin olive oil, the most flavorful and most expensive olive oil, is made from the first pressing of top-quality olives. Full-bodied, fruity, and low in acid, it's best for use in recipes where the flavor can be appreciated, as in salad dressings, or to season foods in the final stages of cooking. "Olive oil" or "pure olive oil," more refined and less flavorful, is used for cooking, because the flavor of extra-virgin oil dissipates somewhat when heated. Olive oils vary according to growing areas, grade, and quality; their color tells little about them. Conduct your own taste test to find the one you like best.

ADVANCE PREPARATION The sauce will keep for up to 3 days in a covered container in the refrigerator.

pita crisps

MAKES 16

This recipe multiplies easily, so you can have baskets brimming with the tasty triangles to accompany your appetizers. They're a quick-to-prepare alternative to packaged crackers.

- **One 6- or 7-inch plain pita bread round, split horizontally (see Tips)**
- **Olive oil for brushing**
- **1 teaspoon dried oregano (see Tips)**
- **2 tablespoons freshly grated Parmesan cheese**

preheat the broiler. Arrange the pita bread halves, rough-side up, on a baking sheet. Lightly brush with oil. Sprinkle with the oregano and Parmesan. Using kitchen shears, cut each pita half into 8 triangles.

broil for about 2 minutes, or until the triangles are lightly browned and the cheese is melted. Watch closely. Serve warm or at room temperature.

tips Lebanese pita bread is flat, with no opening in the middle. Mediterranean or Greek pita bread splits horizontally to form a pocket for stuffing. Pita bread, or pocket bread, is available in Middle Eastern markets and in most supermarkets.

Dried herbs will remain flavorful for about 1 year when stored in a tightly closed container (rather than in a box) in a dark, dry place. It's a good idea to date the jars when you buy them. The herbs should resemble the color they were when fresh and should not be dull or brownish green. To get the most out of your dried herbs, crumble them between your fingers to release the aromatics as you add them to recipes.

VARIATIONS Substitute other dried herbs, such as basil, for the oregano.

Rather than cutting the pita halves into triangles, cut them into 1-inch strips to form "pita pretzels."

ADVANCE PREPARATION These crisps are best when prepared just before serving. They will keep for up to 2 days in a covered container in the refrigerator. If necessary, restore crispness by heating them in a preheated 350°F oven for about 5 minutes.

crostini

(vegan recipe, depending on ingredients in bread)

Crispy Italian toasts, crostini are traditionally browned over a wood-burning fire to kiss them with smoke. Less romantic, but easier, we toast them in the oven. Try them spread with fresh, white, goat cheese topped with strips of Roasted Red Bell Peppers (page 21), or as a foundation for Caesar Crostini (page 71), or munch on them with a few olives and a bite of cheese.

preheat the oven to 400°F. Cut a French baguette into ⅜-inch-thick slices. Lightly brush olive oil (see Tip, page 22) on both sides of each bread slice. Arrange the slices in a single layer on a baking sheet. Bake for about 2 minutes on each side, or until golden brown but not firm all the way through. Serve at room temperature.

tip Store all olive oils in a cool, dark place and use within 1 year. Refrigerate the oil during hot weather. It will become thick and cloudy but this does not affect the flavor or quality; simply bring the oil to room temperature before using to restore the clarity.

ADVANCE PREPARATION Crostini will keep for up to 3 days in an airtight container at room temperature.

wonton wedges

Top these noisy noshes with Roasted Red Pepper Hummus (page 43), Moroccan Carrot Spread (page 44), or Mixed Mushroom–Almond Pâté (page 82).

preheat the oven to 375°F. Lightly brush a baking sheet (or several if you are using lots of wonton skins) with butter. Cut a stack of wonton skins (see Tip) in half diagonally. Place the triangles in a single layer on the prepared sheets. Brush the tops lightly with butter. Sprinkle lightly with freshly grated Parmesan cheese or dried herbs (such as basil, oregano, or thyme), or leave plain.

bake for about 4 to 5 minutes, or until golden brown. Remove from the baking sheets and transfer to a wire rack to cool.

---

tip Wonton skins are thin, square or round sheets of dough made from flour, eggs, and salt. They can be purchased refrigerated in some supermarkets and in Asian markets.

ADVANCE PREPARATION The wedges will keep for up to 2 days in an airtight container at room temperature or in the refrigerator.

bagel chips

(vegan recipe, depending on ingredients in bagels)

A super recipe for day-old bagels. I like to use a variety, such as plain, sun-dried-tomato, and onion bagels. Serve with Roasted Red Pepper Hummus (page 43) or Mixed Mushroom–Almond Pâté (page 82).

preheat the oven to 375°F. Using a serrated knife, cut each bagel into six ¼-inch-thick horizontal slices. Place the slices in a single layer on a baking sheet.

toast the slices in the oven for about 6 to 8 minutes (depending on the moistness of the bagels), turning once, or until lightly browned on both sides and crisp. Break the toasted rounds into smaller chips.

ADVANCE PREPARATION The chips will keep for up to 1 week in an airtight container at room temperature.

crispy tortilla triangles

(vegan recipe, depending on ingredients in tortillas)

These are so fresh, you'll think you're in a Mexican cantina. Top with Mango-Pomegranate Salsa (page 55) or Mixed Mushroom–Almond Pâté (page 82), or use to scoop up Spicy Black Bean Spread (page 40) or Guacamole (page 17).

preheat the broiler. Cut 7-inch flour tortillas into quarters (or more, if you prefer smaller triangles); lightly brush both sides with olive oil. Place them on a baking sheet (see Tip) and prick the surfaces in several places with a fork. Broil 4 to 5 inches from the heat source for about 1 to 2 minutes on each side, or until lightly browned. Watch closely.

transfer to a plate and set aside. (The chips will become crisper as they cool.)

tip When buying baking sheets, select stainless steel instead of aluminum. Aluminum sheets bend and buckle when reheated, resulting in an uneven surface.

VARIATIONS Rather than cutting the tortillas into triangles, use a cookie cutter to cut them into rounds.

Rather than broiling, the triangles or rounds can be baked in a preheated 400°F oven for about 6 minutes. Turn the baking sheet back to front halfway through the baking time.

ADVANCE PREPARATION The chips will keep for up to 2 days in an airtight container at room temperature.

croustades

(vegan recipe, depending on ingredients in bread)

Croustades are cute little edible cups for serving appetizers. Use thinly sliced, white sandwich bread that is very fresh and moist. (I usually purchase the bread at a bakery, where it can be thinly and evenly sliced.) Fill the cups with your choice of warm or room-temperature filling. Try coarsely chopped Roasted Vegetable Antipasto and drizzle the filled cups with Lemon-Caper Sauce (page 76), or stuff the cups with Herbed Diced Vegetables (page 97) or shredded romaine hearts with Caesar Dressing (page 71).

preheat the oven to 350°F. Use a serrated knife to cut a fresh, moist, white sandwich bread loaf into ¼-inch-thick slices. Use a cookie cutter, the rim of a glass, or a knife to cut the bread slices into 3-inch rounds. Gently press the rounds into mini-muffin cups (about 2 inches in diameter). Bake for about 10 minutes, or until the bread shells are lightly browned. Let cool in the pan on a wire rack.

ADVANCE PREPARATION The croustades can be made up to 1 day in advance. Cover and store in a tin or plastic container at room temperature.

toast points

(vegan recipe, depending on ingredients in bread)

These simple homemade creations are better than packaged toasts. Use them as a base for thin layers of crème fraîche, finely crumbled hard-cooked egg, and Black-Olive Caviar (page 32); simply top them with Basil Pesto (page 16) or Blue Cheese Spread (page 42); or serve them as a crunchy accompaniment to other appetizers.

preheat the oven to 300°F. Cut a loaf of fresh, moist, white sandwich bread into ¼-inch-thick slices. Using a serrated knife in a sawing motion, trim the crusts off the bread, then cut each slice in half on the diagonal. Arrange the triangles on a baking sheet. Bake for about 5 minutes on each side, or until dry and lightly toasted.

VARIATIONS Rather than cutting the bread slices into triangles, use a cookie cutter to cut them into shapes, such as hearts, stars, or rounds.

Grill the triangles (or other shapes) on a dry stovetop grill pan or on an outdoor grill for about 3 to 5 minutes on each side, or until light grill marks show.

ADVANCE PREPARATION The toasts will keep for up to 1 week in a covered container in the refrigerator or may be frozen for up to 6 months.

toasted tortilla cups

(vegan recipe, depending on ingredients in tortillas)

Crispy cups of flour or corn tortillas make edible containers to wow your guests. Freshly made tortillas from a specialty market are the best, but packaged tortillas from the supermarket will work, too. Try garlic-, basil-, and jalapeño-flavored flour tortillas, now available at most markets, along with tortillas colored with tomatoes or spinach. For an out-of-the-ordinary presentation, serve the filled cups atop a layer of uncooked dried black beans on a colorful tray.

preheat the oven to 350°F. Use a cookie cutter, the rim of a glass, or a knife to cut flour or corn tortillas into 3-inch rounds. (You can cut 3 rounds from each 10-inch burrito-size tortilla.)

to prevent the tortillas from cracking as they are bent, soften the rounds: Place them between 2 moistened paper towels and microwave on high for about 20 seconds, or until warm and soft. Or, wrap the tortillas in aluminum foil and heat in a 350°F oven for about 5 minutes. Cover to keep warm.

firmly press the warm, soft rounds into lightly oiled mini-muffin cups (about 2 inches in diameter). Lightly brush with olive oil. Bake for 8 to 10 minutes, or until firm and crispy. Let cool in the pan on a wire rack.

serve with your choice of room-temperature or warm filling. For example, fill the cups with Mango-Pomegranate Salsa (page 55) or Spicy Black Bean Spread (page 40) layered with finely shredded lettuce, shredded cheese, and sour cream. Or, fill the cups with a layer of Guacamole (page 17) topped with Red Pepper–Corn Salsa (page 18) or Apple Salsa (page 73). Delicious warm fillings are Cumin-Scented Potatoes (page 91) or Herbed Diced Vegetables (page 97).

VARIATION Use packaged wonton skins to make appetizer cups; no need to heat them first, because they are already soft. Bake molded wonton skins for about 5 minutes, or until firm and lightly browned.

ADVANCE PREPARATION The tortilla (or wonton) cups will keep for up to 2 days in an airtight container at room temperature. Fill cups up to 1 hour before serving.

LIGHT BITES

These nibbles and noshes will have even your most sophisticated guests licking their fingers and trying just one more. Who can refuse elegant Quail Eggs with Olivada (page 36) or more-casual Moroccan Carrot Spread with Pita (page 44)? Plates aren't always necessary here, but do offer plenty of napkins. These bites are light on the palate, introducing a meal or adding to more substantial appetizer fare.

Use a food processor (or blender) to quickly whip dips and spreads, scraping down the sides occasionally as the ingredients blend to ensure smooth textures. If you are using a blender, it may be necessary to process the ingredients in several small batches.

These dips and spreads keep well in the refrigerator, actually mellowing and improving as the flavors blend. Some can be used as components in more artistically arranged presentations.

black-olive caviar light bites

MAKES 48 (½ CUP CAVIAR)

Polish the sterling or grab a selection of colorful plastic spoons; this lovely appetizer demands a tasty presentation. It's my favorite way to show off those unmatched sterling silver spoons from a Paris flea market. Once assembled, arrange the spoons on a tray or platter and circulate among the guests. Serve Toast Points (page 29) or Crostini (page 24) as an accompaniment.

BLACK-OLIVE CAVIAR:

One 2¼-ounce can sliced black olives, drained and finely chopped
1 tablespoon minced fresh basil
2 teaspoons balsamic vinegar (see Tip)
2 teaspoons extra-virgin olive oil
1 clove garlic, minced, or ½ teaspoon prepared minced garlic
⅛ teaspoon red pepper flakes, or to taste
⅛ teaspoon freshly ground pepper, or to taste

TO COMPLETE THE RECIPE:

1 hard-cooked egg (see Tip, page 85)
Salt and freshly ground pepper to taste
½ cup crème fraîche, sour cream, or fresh, white goat cheese

to make the caviar: Stir together all the caviar ingredients in a small bowl. Taste and adjust the seasoning.

using a fork, finely crumble the egg in a small bowl. Season to taste.

to assemble each serving: Starting at the handle end of the bowl of each spoon, arrange a row of about ½ teaspoon crème fraîche, sour cream, or goat cheese, about ½ teaspoon egg, and about ½ teaspoon caviar.

to serve: Pass the assembled spoons on a tray or platter. Provide a glass or other container where your guests can place the spoons once they have taken their bite.

continued »

tip Balsamic vinegar, the Italian *aceto balsamico,* is a wine vinegar made by boiling the juice of white Trebbiano grapes in copper pots until it caramelizes. The vinegar is then aged for up to thirty years in barrels made from various woods (oak, chestnut, mulberry, and juniper), each adding a hint of its woody flavor. The result is a vinegar with a heavy, mellow, almost-sweet flavor and a dark color.

Commercially produced balsamic vinegar, available in most supermarkets, is regular vinegar to which boiled-down grapes, caramelized sugar, and other flavoring and coloring ingredients have been added (along with, in some cases, a little real *aceto balsamico*). Store balsamic vinegar in a cool, dark place for up to 6 months after opening.

VARIATION Layer the ingredients in Crisp New Potato Cups (page 97) in this order: egg, crème fraîche, caviar.

ADVANCE PREPARATION The caviar will keep for up to 2 days in a covered container in the refrigerator. Assemble the spoons up to 1 hour before serving; cover and refrigerate.

red potato and black-olive caviar canapés

MAKES 30

Crisp potato slices, smooth cream, and spicy and salty olives all in a single bite. Substitute cucumber slices for the potato slices to make an even lighter bite.

POTATO DISKS:

6 small (2-inch) red potatoes, scrubbed but not peeled
2 tablespoons olive oil
Salt and freshly ground pepper to taste

CANAPÉ LAYERS:

⅔ cup crème fraîche (see Tips), sour cream, or room-temperature fresh, white goat cheese
1 recipe Black-Olive Caviar (page 32)
Minced fresh chives for garnish (see Tips)

to make the potato disks: Preheat the oven to 375°F. Trim the ends off the potatoes and discard. Cut the potatoes into ¼-inch-thick slices. Toss the potatoes with the olive oil in a small bowl.

arrange the slices on a baking sheet and sprinkle with salt and pepper. Bake for about 20 to 25 minutes, or until the potato slices are lightly browned. Let cool.

to assemble the canapés: Spread each potato slice with about 1 teaspoon crème fraîche, sour cream, or goat cheese. Top with 1 teaspoon of the Black-Olive Caviar and sprinkle with chives.

tips Crème fraîche is a thickened cream, sold in the dairy section of gourmet markets and some supermarkets. It's tangy, smooth, and rich.

Chives are a member of the onion family, with a mild onion taste. If possible, buy potted chives or grow them in your garden. Use scissors to snip off what you need, cutting off whole blades rather than chopping the tops off all the blades. If you buy cut chives, wrap them in damp paper towels, seal in a plastic bag, and refrigerate for up to 1 week.

ADVANCE PREPARATION Bake the potato slices up to 2 hours before serving. Assemble the canapés just before serving.

quail eggs with olivada

MAKES 24 (⅓ CUP OLIVADA)

These tiny eggs look lovely on small, baby spinach leaves. Olivada is my favorite topping, but for simplicity, you can simply top the egg halves with thin strips of kalamata olives or minced fresh chives; or you can combine the yolks with mayonnaise and a dash of salt and pepper to make miniature deviled eggs. Keep a few of the boiled mottled-shelled eggs intact for garnishing the plate.

15 quail eggs (see Tip)

OLIVADA:

¼ cup finely chopped canned black olives
1 tablespoon extra-virgin olive oil
2 teaspoons fresh lemon juice
1 tablespoon minced fresh chives
Red pepper flakes to taste
Salt and freshly ground pepper to taste

TO COMPLETE THE RECIPE:

24 capers, rinsed and patted dry
Tips of fresh thyme sprigs for garnish
24 baby spinach leaves

put the quail eggs in a small saucepan and cover with cold water. Bring the water to a boil over high heat. As the water heats, occasionally stir the eggs gently. Reduce the heat to medium and cook the eggs for 3 minutes, occasionally stirring gently. (Stirring will keep the yolks in the centers of the boiled eggs.)

using a slotted spoon, transfer the eggs to a pan of cold water. Let stand until completely cool, about 3 minutes. (The cold water bath will prevent the peeled eggs from having flat ends.)

meanwhile, make the Olivada: Process all the olivada ingredients in a food processor (or blender) until smooth.

continued »

lightly tap each egg on all sides on a hard surface, then use the palm of your hand to roll it gently. When the shell begins to crack, carefully peel the egg, removing both the membrane and the attached shell.

using a sharp knife, halve 12 of the eggs lengthwise. Between eggs, wipe the knife blade with a damp towel to remove any yolk that clings.

lightly sprinkle each egg half (yolk-side up) with pepper. Top each with about ¼ teaspoon of the Olivada. Top with a caper and an herb sprig. Arrange the eggs on a plate atop individual spinach leaves.

spoon any extra Olivada into a small bowl to serve as a spread for crackers or Crostini (page 24).

tip Quail eggs are about one third the size of a chicken's egg, and they have speckled beige shells. They can be purchased in specialty and Asian markets. Check the freshness expiration date on the package and refrigerate the eggs in their container.

ADVANCE PREPARATION Olivada will keep for up to 2 days in a covered container in the refrigerator. The eggs can be cooked up to 1 day in advance and refrigerated. Once peeled, the eggs can be held for up to 6 hours in an airtight container in the refrigerator. Slice the eggs and assemble up to 1 hour before serving. Serve at room temperature.

pistachio-crusted creamy goat cheese round

MAKES ½ TO ¾ CUP (ENOUGH FOR ABOUT 12 CROSTINI)

Serve this delectably warm and creamy cheese on your favorite platter, surrounded with Crostini (page 24), Bagel Chips (page 26), or Crispy Tortilla Triangles (page 27).

- One 4- to 6-ounce log fresh, white goat cheese (see Tip)
- 2 tablespoons finely crushed pistachio nuts
- 1 tablespoon finely crushed garlic- and herb-flavored dried bread crumbs
- 1 teaspoon extra-virgin olive oil
- Fresh rosemary sprigs for garnish

preheat the broiler. Form the cheese log into a flattened round about 4 inches in diameter and ½ inch thick. Transfer to an ovenproof plate or shallow bowl.

combine the nuts, bread crumbs, and olive oil in a small bowl. Spread over the cheese round and press gently.

broil 4 to 5 inches from the heat source for about 1½ minutes, or until the coating is lightly browned and the cheese is bubbly around the edges.

garnish with rosemary sprigs and serve warm. Provide small knives for spreading.

---

tip Goat cheese, known as *chèvre* in French, is made from goat's milk and may be either white or coated with herbs. Once opened, wrap the cheese in plastic wrap and store in the refrigerator for up to 2 weeks.

ADVANCE PREPARATION The cheese round can be assembled with the nut mixture early in the day; cover and refrigerate. Broil just before serving.

spicy black bean spread

MAKES 1 CUP *(vegan recipe)*

In a pinch? This black bean dip is ready in a blink. If you have a chance, assemble individual canapés using Crispy Tortilla Triangles (page 27). Top each triangle with about 1 teaspoon of the spread and 1 teaspoon finely shredded Monterey Jack, Colby, or Cheddar cheese; broil for about 1 minute, or until the cheese melts. Top each canapé with about ½ teaspoon sour cream and a small piece of red bell pepper.

1 tablespoon olive oil
¼ cup coarsely chopped onion
2 cloves garlic, minced, or 1 teaspoon prepared minced garlic
One 15-ounce can black beans, drained and rinsed
2 tablespoons fresh lime juice
1 tablespoon minced jalapeño chile, or to taste
¼ teaspoon ground cumin
Salt and freshly ground pepper to taste
3 tablespoons coarsely chopped fresh cilantro

heat the oil in a small nonstick skillet over medium-high heat. Add the onion and garlic; cook, stirring occasionally, until tender, about 4 minutes.

process the beans, lime juice, chile, cumin, salt, pepper, and the onion mixture in a food processor until smooth. Stir in the cilantro. Taste and adjust the seasoning.

---

tip Vegetable leaves, such as lettuce and spinach, and large-leafed herbs, such as basil, can be cut into shreds, sometimes called a *chiffonade*. Stack the leaves on a cutting board and roll the pile cigar-style, then slice across the roll to make fine strips.

VARIATION Use the spread as a filling for Toasted Tortilla Cups (page 30): When making the spread, reserve ½ cup of the beans; stir them in after puréeing to make the spread chunky. Spread a thin layer of finely shredded lettuce (see Tip) in the bottom of each cup, top with Spicy Black Bean Spread, Red Pepper–Corn Salsa (page 18), or a dollop of sour cream.

ADVANCE PREPARATION The spread will keep for up to 1 week in a covered container in the refrigerator.

roasted red pepper–cheese spread

MAKES 1½ CUPS

Take it from the pros: A cream syringe or pastry bag fitted with a small star tip will pipe perfect swirls of creamy spread into celery, cherry tomatoes, and bright green, blanched sugar pea pods. Or, make a container for the spread from a hollowed-out red or green bell pepper and pair with Crostini (page 24), Bagel Chips (page 26), or crackers.

- **1 cup (4 ounces) finely shredded Cheddar cheese**
- **½ cup coarsely chopped Roasted Red Bell Pepper (page 21), or jarred roasted red bell pepper, well drained**
- **¼ cup cottage cheese**
- **¼ cup sour cream**
- **¼ teaspoon Tabasco sauce, or to taste (see Tip)**
- **Salt and freshly ground pepper to taste**

process all the ingredients in a food processor (or blender) until smooth. Taste and adjust the seasoning.

tip Refrigerate Tabasco sauce after opening to retain its flavor and red color.

VARIATION To make a sun-dried tomato spread, substitute chopped, well-drained, oil-packed sun-dried tomatoes for the roasted red bell pepper.

ADVANCE PREPARATION The spread will keep for up to 3 days in a covered container in the refrigerator.

blue cheese spread

MAKES 1¼ CUPS

Offer bunches of juicy red grapes next to a bowl of this dip. Blue cheese and grapes make a stunning duo. For an impressive presentation, trim to flatten both ends of seedless red grapes and scoop out part of the inside with a tiny baller (available in kitchenware shops). With a cream syringe or pastry bag fitted with a tiny star tip, pipe a bit of spread into each grape; chill until the filling sets. Arrange the grapes atop a fresh or paper grape leaf on a plate. If time is short, stuff just a few grapes to use as a garnish and serve this salty spread with Crostini (page 24), Pita Crisps (page 23), toasted party rye, or a basket of crispy garlic-flavored breadsticks for dipping.

½ cup (4 ounces) cream cheese, at room temperature
½ cup crumbled blue cheese
¼ cup sour cream
½ cup finely chopped green onions (white and green parts); see Tip
Freshly ground pepper to taste

process all the ingredients in a food processor (or blender) until smooth. Add pepper to taste.

tip Green onions, also called scallions, are delicate members of the onion family. Their size varies from very slender to thick; as a rule, the narrower the onion, the sweeter the flavor. The white part should be firm and unblemished; the leaves should be bright green and firm. Both parts can be used in most recipes calling for green onions. Wrap green onions in a plastic bag and store them for up to 1 week in the vegetable-crisper section of the refrigerator.

VARIATION Stir 2 tablespoons finely chopped walnuts into the spread. Serve with apple, pear, or fresh fig slices.

ADVANCE PREPARATION The spread will keep for up to 3 days in a covered container in the refrigerator.

roasted red pepper hummus

MAKES 1¼ CUPS *(vegan recipe)*

This spread is one of my favorites to have on hand, a must for quick canapés of sliced cucumber, to stuff into hollowed-out cherry tomatoes, or to spread in chunks of celery. For a "sizable bite," stir in diced cucumber, diced red onion, and minced cilantro and serve in endive leaves.

- 1 tablespoon olive oil
- ¼ cup finely chopped onion (see Tips)
- 4 cloves garlic, minced, or 2 teaspoons prepared minced garlic
- One 15-ounce can Great Northern beans, drained and rinsed
- 1 tablespoon fresh lemon juice
- ½ cup coarsely chopped Roasted Red Bell Pepper (page 21), or jarred roasted red bell pepper, well drained
- ¼ teaspoon freshly ground pepper, or to taste
- Pinch of red pepper flakes, or to taste
- Salt to taste
- Fresh basil or cilantro sprigs for garnish

heat the oil in a small nonstick skillet over medium heat. Add the onion and garlic and cook, stirring occasionally, until the onion is translucent, about 3 minutes. Remove from the heat and set aside.

combine the beans, lemon juice, and bell pepper in a food processor (or blender). Add the onion mixture and all the remaining ingredients except the herb sprigs; process until smooth. Taste and adjust the seasoning.

let stand at room temperature for about 1 hour before serving. Garnish with herb sprigs and serve.

---

tips White and yellow onions will keep 2 months stored in a cool, dry, dark place with good air circulation. Red onions keep 2 to 4 weeks. Stored in the refrigerator, onions keep 1 week.

If you need only part of an onion, do not peel before cutting. The unused portion keeps better in the refrigerator if the skin is left on. Store in a screw-top jar, and use within 4 days.

Tear-producing vapors can be reduced by refrigerating an onion for several hours or by freezing it for 20 minutes before chopping.

ADVANCE PREPARATION Flavors will blend if the spread is made 1 or 2 days in advance; cover and refrigerate for up to 1 week.

moroccan carrot spread with pita

MAKES ABOUT 24 (1¼ CUPS SPREAD) *(vegan recipe, depending on ingredients in pita bread rounds)*

Vibrant and colorful, this creamy spread relies on carrots cooked until very, very tender. Spread on pitas or enjoy as a dip for raw vegetables.

CARROT SPREAD:

1 pound (about 6) carrots, cut into 1-inch chunks
3 tablespoons extra-virgin olive oil
3 tablespoons red wine vinegar
2 cloves garlic, minced, or 1 teaspoon prepared minced garlic
1 teaspoon sweet Hungarian paprika, or to taste (see Tip)
2 teaspoons ground cumin seeds
½ teaspoon minced fresh ginger

TO COMPLETE THE RECIPE:

Four 6- or 7-inch plain pita bread rounds
Minced fresh flat-leaf parsley and coarsely chopped black olives or halved kalamata olives for garnish

to make the spread: Steam the carrots over boiling water until very tender, 14 to 16 minutes. Or, put them in a medium, microwave-proof dish; add ¼ cup water. Cover and microwave on high for 10 to 12 minutes. Drain well and let cool.

process the carrots in a food processor (or blender) until mashed. Add all the remaining spread ingredients, process until smooth and creamy. Taste and adjust the seasoning. Cool to room temperature.

to serve, spread about ⅓ cup Carrot Spread over each pita bread round; sprinkle with parsley. Cut into 6 wedges; top each with chopped olives.

tip Paprika is a powder made from ground, sweet red pepper pods. The flavor ranges from mild to pungent and hot, and the color from red-orange to deep red. To preserve its color and flavor, paprika should be stored in a cool, dark place for no longer than 6 months.

ADVANCE PREPARATION The spread will keep for up to 3 days in a covered container in the refrigerator. Bring to room temperature before serving.

lebne with zaatar (middle eastern herbed yogurt cheese)

MAKES 1 CUP

According to my friend Cynthia Myntti, who has spent many years working and traveling in the Middle East, tangy, fresh yogurt cheese (*lebne*) is a "must" on the *mezze,* or appetizer, platter in those regions. Seasoned with toasted sesame seeds, dried thyme (*zaatar* in Arabic), coriander, chopped pistachios, and sumac berries, then drizzled with olive oil, it is a tribute to ancient flavors. You'll need to plan ahead to prepare the cheese 1 day in advance. Serve the seasoned cheese with crackers, wedges of pita bread (preferably Lebanese pita bread with no pocket), Pita Crisps (page 23), or Crostini (page 24) and a bowl of imported olives.

YOGURT CHEESE:

2 cups fresh plain yogurt (do not use yogurt with gelatin added)

SEASONING MIXTURE:

1 tablespoon toasted sesame seeds (see Tip, page 50)
½ teaspoon dried thyme
½ teaspoon dried summer savory
¼ teaspoon cayenne pepper
¼ teaspoon ground sumac, optional (see Tip)
¼ teaspoon ground cumin
¼ teaspoon salt

TO COMPLETE THE RECIPE:

2 tablespoons extra-virgin olive oil

to make the yogurt cheese: Set a strainer over a deep medium bowl, making certain the strainer does not touch the bottom of the bowl. Line the strainer with 4 layers of cheesecloth, allowing about 4 inches to extend over the sides of the strainer, or line with a paper coffee filter.

spoon the yogurt into the strainer. If using cheesecloth, gather the ends and fold them over the yogurt. Cover the strainer and bowl with plastic wrap to prevent the surface of the yogurt cheese from drying out. Refrigerate for at least 8 hours or overnight.

transfer the thickened yogurt cheese to a small serving bowl; discard the cheesecloth or paper filter and the liquid.

to make the seasoning mixture: Combine all the seasoning ingredients in a small bowl.

to serve, drizzle the yogurt cheese with the olive oil and sprinkle with the seasoning mixture. Serve chilled or at room temperature.

tip Penzeys Spices, a mail-order company, offers a wide variety of spices and dried herbs, including ground sumac and a premixed seasoning blend for making Lebne with Zaatar. For more information, call 1-800-741-7787 or visit www.penzeys.com.

ADVANCE PREPARATION Begin this recipe at least 8 hours before serving. The yogurt cheese will keep for up to 1 week in a covered container in the refrigerator. Top with the olive oil and seasoning mixture just before serving.

asparagus with toasted sesame aioli

MAKES 16 (⅓ CUP AIOLI)

Paris kisses Saigon in this heavenly aioli. Here bold, toasty sesame oil adds depth to the classic French garlic-lemon mayonnaise. Arrange the crisp-tender asparagus spears, tips up, in a tall, clear glass, with the sesame sauce nearby, served in a radicchio leaf cup for color.

16 medium-thick asparagus spears (about 12 ounces), trimmed to even lengths (see Tips)

TOASTED SESAME AIOLI:

¼ cup mayonnaise
1 tablespoon Asian sesame oil (see Tips)
2 teaspoons soy sauce
2 teaspoons fresh lemon juice
1 teaspoon toasted sesame seeds (see Tips)
½ teaspoon minced fresh ginger
1 clove garlic, minced, or ½ teaspoon prepared minced garlic

TO COMPLETE THE RECIPE:

1 radicchio leaf (optional)
Additional toasted sesame seeds for garnish

steam the asparagus in a covered steamer over boiling water until crisp-tender, about 4 minutes. Or, put the asparagus in a microwave-proof dish; add about 2 tablespoons water. Cover tightly and microwave on high for about 3 minutes. Drain well. Rinse with cold water and drain again.

meanwhile, make the aioli: Stir together all the aioli ingredients in a small bowl until smooth.

to serve, arrange the asparagus spears in a tall, clear glass container. Spoon the sauce into a radicchio leaf or a small dish, garnish with sesame seeds, and place nearby for dipping.

continued ››

tips Asparagus is at its best in the early spring; however, it is available year-round in most markets. Choose green spears with firm stalks; the tips should be tightly closed and have a lavender hue. To store, wrap in a plastic bag and store in the vegetable crisper; use within 2 to 3 days. If wilted, stand the stalks in a jar filled with 2 inches of very cold water. Cover with a plastic bag, seal,and refrigerate for 1 to 2 hours before cooking.

Buy dark, amber-colored Asian sesame oil, made from toasted sesame seeds, rather than light-colored sesame oil, which is extracted from raw sesame seeds and lacks the distinctive strong aroma and nutty flavor. Purchase Asian sesame oil in the Asian section of supermarkets or in Asian markets. After opening, store it in the refrigerator, where it will keep for up to 6 months.

Toasting gives sesame seeds a slightly crispy texture and a nutty flavor. Put the seeds in a dry skillet over medium-high heat and toss constantly until they are lightly browned, about 3 to 5 minutes. Or, toast them on a jelly-roll pan in a preheated 350°F oven for about 10 minutes. Shake the pan or stir the seeds occasionally while toasting. Immediately transfer the seeds to a bowl. It takes the same amount of time to toast 1 tablespoon or ½ cup, so toast extra seeds, store them in an airtight container, and refrigerate or freeze for up to 6 months.

ADVANCE PREPARATION The asparagus can be cooked up to 1 day in advance. The sauce will keep for up to 1 week in a covered container in the refrigerator. Bring both to room temperature for serving.

chutney–hot chile tortilla canapés

MAKES 24 *(vegan recipe, depending on ingredients in tortilla chips)*

A sweet-hot play on crisp tortillas, this dynamite crowd-pleaser can be ready in minutes using your favorite tortilla chips and chutney from the supermarket. No one can eat just one.

24 bite-sized round white corn tortilla chips
3 tablespoons mango chutney
2 tablespoons finely chopped red onion
1 tablespoon minced fresh cilantro
1 teaspoon minced Thai or jalapeño chile, or to taste (see Tips)

spread each chip with about ½ teaspoon of the chutney. Combine all the remaining ingredients in a small bowl. Spoon about ½ teaspoon of the mixture atop the chutney in the center of each chip.

tips Just how hot a chile is depends on the amount of a substance called capsaicin (kap-SAY-ih-sihn), found mainly in the veins near the seeds. Unaffected by heat or cold, capsaicin retains its potency despite time, cooking, or freezing, so removing the membranes and seeds before using chilies is the only way to reduce the heat. Small chilies have more membranes and seeds than large ones, so generally they are hotter.

To avoid irritation from the caustic oils in chilies, do not touch your eyes, nose, or lips while handling them. Many cooks wear disposable plastic gloves when working with chilies. Afterward, wash your hands, knife, and cutting board in hot, soapy water.

ADVANCE PREPARATION The canapés can be assembled up to 2 hours before serving; arrange them in a single layer on a plate, cover, and refrigerate.

roasted red pepper- and feta-stuffed zucchini cups

MAKES ABOUT 16

Make these ahead, but broil them right before serving. The aromas will draw everyone to the platter, so make a few extras. Serve the stuffing in Crisp New Potato Cups (page 97) for larger bites.

ZUCCHINI CUPS:

2 zucchini, each about 8 inches long

ROASTED RED PEPPER AND FETA STUFFING:

⅓ cup minced Roasted Red Bell Pepper (page 21), or jarred roasted red bell pepper, well drained

⅓ cup coarsely crumbled feta cheese (see Tips)

2 tablespoons toasted pine nuts (see Tip, page 16)

1 teaspoon minced fresh oregano, or ¼ teaspoon dried oregano (see Tips)

⅛ teaspoon freshly ground pepper, or to taste

preheat the broiler. Lightly oil a small shallow baking pan.

to make the zucchini cups: Trim and discard the zucchini ends. Cut the zucchini crosswise into ¾-inch-thick slices. Using a melon baller, scoop out the center of each slice, leaving a shell a little less than ¼ inch thick. Steam the cups in a covered steamer over boiling water until just barely tender, about 4 minutes. Or, pour about 2 tablespoons water into the bottom of a flat-bottomed, medium, microwave-proof dish. Arrange the cups in the dish in a single layer, scooped-side up. Cover tightly and microwave for about 2 minutes. Drain the cups upside down on a plate lined with a paper towel.

to make the stuffing: Stir together all the stuffing ingredients in a small bowl. Taste and adjust the seasoning.

to serve, transfer the zucchini cups to the prepared pan and mound some of the stuffing in each. Broil about 4 inches from the heating element for about 3 minutes, or until the cheese is softened and lightly browned. Serve warm.

continued ››

tips Feta cheese is a white Greek cheese with a tangy flavor. Traditionally, it is made with goat's milk, sheep's milk, or a combination; today, it is often made with cow's milk. You can either crumble the block of cheese using your fingers or buy a package of crumbled feta.

Fresh herbs, which come from the leafy part of plants, contain more moisture and therefore are milder in taste than dried herbs. When substituting, use 3 to 4 times more fresh herbs than dried.

ADVANCE PREPARATION Steam the zucchini cups and stuff them up to 6 hours before broiling; cover and refrigerate. Broil just before serving.

mango-pomegranate salsa with crispy tortilla triangles

MAKES 16 (ABOUT 1½ CUPS SALSA) *(vegan recipe, depending on ingredients in tortillas)*

In Antalya, Turkey, the pomegranates are so plentiful that street vendors mound them in piles on the ground. On a recent visit, I couldn't drink enough of their vibrant, red juice. In this recipe, the seeds burst their sweet-tart flavor into the creamy mango, and the color is wild. I like to top Crispy Tortilla Triangles with the salsa; but for more casual entertaining, provide a bowl of salsa and a basket of triangles, so your guests can assemble their own.

MANGO-POMEGRANATE SALSA:

- 1 mango, peeled and cut into ⅜-inch cubes (see Tips)
- ¼ cup pomegranate seeds (see Tips)
- 1 green onion (green part only), finely chopped
- 1 tablespoon dried currants
- 2 tablespoons minced fresh cilantro
- 1 tablespoon fresh lime juice
- 1 teaspoon minced jalapeño chile, or to taste
- 1 clove garlic, minced, or ½ teaspoon prepared minced garlic
- Salt and freshly ground pepper to taste

TO COMPLETE THE RECIPE:

- 16 Crispy Tortilla Triangles (page 27)

to make the salsa: Stir together the mango, pomegranate seeds, green onion, and currants in a medium bowl. Whisk together all the remaining salsa ingredients in a small bowl; add to the mango mixture and toss gently. Taste and adjust the seasoning.

to serve, spoon about 1 tablespoon of the salsa on each tortilla triangle. Serve at room temperature.

continued »

tips The simplest method for pitting a mango is to hold it horizontally, then cut it in two lengthwise, slightly off-center, so the knife just misses the pit. Repeat the cut on the other side so a thin layer of flesh remains around the flat pit. Holding a half, flesh-side up, in the palm of your hand, slash the flesh into a lattice, cutting down to, but not through, the peel. Carefully push the center of the peel upward with your thumbs to turn it inside out, opening the cuts of the flesh. Then cut the mango cubes from the peel.

Pomegranates are available from October through December and can be refrigerated for up to 2 months. To use, cut the fruit in half and pry out the seeds, removing any light-colored membrane that adheres. To simplify the task and avoid splashing juice, submerge each half in a bowl of cold water and tear the flesh apart under water; the seeds will drop to the bottom and the pulp will float. Remove the pulp with a slotted spoon and strain the seeds.

VARIATIONS Omit the pomegranate seeds if they are unavailable. For color, add 2 tablespoons finely chopped red onion.

Serve the salsa, in about 1-tablespoon quantities, in endive leaves rather than on tortilla chips.

ADVANCE PREPARATION The salsa will keep for up to 1 day in a covered container in the refrigerator. Assemble the salsa with the tortilla triangles just before serving.

cherry tomatoes with lemon-walnut pesto stuffing

MAKES 24 (½ CUP PESTO)

The garden's gift to busy cooks is a perfect cherry tomato. These bite-sized treats bring summer to any appetizer tray. Use an array of red and yellow cherry and tiny, pear-shaped tomatoes when they're available.

LEMON-WALNUT PESTO:

½ cup coarsely chopped toasted walnuts (see Tip)
½ cup loosely packed fresh basil leaves
¼ cup freshly grated Parmesan cheese
2 tablespoons extra-virgin olive oil
1 tablespoon fresh lemon juice
¼ teaspoon freshly ground pepper, or to taste
Salt to taste

TO COMPLETE THE RECIPE:

12 cherry tomatoes
Paprika, fresh basil sprigs, and toasted walnut halves (see Tip) for garnish

to make the pesto: Process all the pesto ingredients in a food processor (or blender) until slightly chunky. Taste and adjust the seasoning.

halve the tomatoes horizontally. Using a small melon baller or a spoon, scoop out the seeds and juice. Fill each tomato shell with about 1 teaspoon of the pesto. Sprinkle lightly with paprika just before serving.

to serve, arrange the stuffed tomatoes on a plate and garnish with basil sprigs and walnut halves. Serve chilled or at room temperature.

---

tip Toasting enhances the flavor of most nuts. To toast nuts on the stovetop, toss them in a dry skillet over medium heat until they are golden brown, 4 to 5 minutes. Or, if you prefer, toast them on a jelly-roll pan in a preheated 350°F oven for 8 to 10 minutes.

VARIATION Cut a thin slice to remove the tomato top (with stem attached), scoop out the seeds, fill the shell with pesto, and use the tomato top as a tiny lid.

ADVANCE PREPARATION The pesto will keep for up to 2 days in a covered container in the refrigerator. Stuff the tomatoes up to 4 hours before serving; cover and refrigerate.

asparagus roll-ups

MAKES 18

These canapés have been in my appetizer repertoire for decades. Always good, they're better when made with top-quality bread, thinly sliced at your bakery, and imported blue cheese. I usually double the recipe to have extras on hand in the freezer.

- 6 thick asparagus spears
- ¼ cup (2 ounces) cream cheese, at room temperature
- ¼ cup blue cheese (see Tip)
- 1 egg white
- Six ¼-inch-thick slices white or wheat sandwich bread
- 2 tablespoons unsalted butter, melted

trim the asparagus to be as long as the bread slices. Steam the asparagus in a covered steamer over boiling water until tender. Or, put the asparagus in a microwave-proof dish and add about 1 tablespoon water. Cover tightly and microwave on high for about 4 minutes. Drain well.

combine the cream cheese, blue cheese, and egg white in a small bowl. Trim the crusts off the bread and use a rolling pin to flatten the slices. Spread each slice with about 2 teaspoons of the cheese mixture. Place an asparagus stalk atop the cheese at the edge of the slice and roll to wrap the asparagus.

brush the rolls on all sides with melted butter and place on an ungreased baking sheet. Place the sheet in the freezer for about 15 minutes, or until the bread is almost frozen. Meanwhile, preheat the oven to 400°F.

slice each roll into thirds and bake for about 10 minutes, or until the bread is lightly browned and crispy. Serve warm.

tip Fresh and soft-ripened cheeses should be tightly wrapped; they will keep for up to 2 weeks in the coldest part of the refrigerator. Discard fresh or soft-ripened cheeses that become moldy.

ADVANCE PREPARATION The baked roll-ups can be frozen in a closed container for up to 1 month. Heat the frozen roll-ups in a preheated 350°F oven for about 5 minutes, or until warmed through.

pesto palmiers

MAKES 28 (*vegan recipe if puff pastry is made with oil, and if pesto is made without Parmesan cheese*)

Who says elegance means fuss? Hang in there through this recipe's instructions. With puff pastry and Basil Pesto on hand in the freezer, the procedure is easy once you get started.

1 sheet frozen puff pastry, thawed (see Tips)

⅓ cup Basil Pesto (page 16)

preheat the oven to 400°F. Line a baking sheet with parchment paper (see Tips).

unfold the pastry sheet on a lightly floured surface. Roll with a rolling pin to form an 11-by-16-inch rectangle. With a short side toward you, trim to even the edges. Spoon the pesto onto the center of the rectangle; use a rubber spatula to spread it in a very thin, even layer to the edges of the pastry.

use both hands to gently lift one long edge of the pastry. Fold it firmly and evenly over itself in 1-inch sections until you reach the center of the sheet. Repeat, folding the other edge to meet the center.

cut the double-folded pastry into ⅜-inch-thick slices. Place them about 2 inches apart, cut-side down, on the prepared pan. Bake for about 10 minutes, or until puffed and golden brown. Transfer to a wire rack to cool.

---

tips Puff pastry is a multilayered French pastry that puffs when baked to make light, flaky layers. It is found in the freezer section of most supermarkets. To thaw, let the package sit at room temperature for 20 to 30 minutes. Made-from-scratch puff pastry contains butter, but some packaged puff pastry is made with oil and can be used in vegan recipes.

Parchment paper is a grease- and moisture-resistant paper that can be used to line baking pans, to wrap foods that are to be baked *en papillote,* and to make disposable pastry bags. It is available in gourmet shops and most supermarkets.

ADVANCE PREPARATION Palmiers will keep for up to 3 days in a covered container in the refrigerator or for up to 1 month in the freezer. Recrisp in a preheated 350°F oven for about 5 minutes before serving.

mushroom duxelles pinwheels

MAKES ABOUT 60 (¾ CUP DUXELLES)

Rich and meaty, duxelles is a mixture of finely chopped mushrooms, shallots, and herbs, simmered in butter and cooked until thick and fragrant. Here it is rolled in a nut-studded pastry. You may also serve the duxelles with Toast Points (page 29) or spread it on Crostini (page 24), top with strips of Roasted Red Bell Peppers (page 21), and garnish with tiny, fresh thyme sprigs.

NUT PASTRY:

2 cups unbleached all-purpose flour
¾ cup (1½ sticks) cold unsalted butter, cut into 1-inch pieces
¼ cup coarsely chopped walnuts or pecans, ground
½ teaspoon salt
1 egg
1 teaspoon fresh lemon juice
1 tablespoon ice water, or as needed

MUSHROOM DUXELLES:

3 tablespoons unsalted butter, divided
¼ cup minced shallots (see Tip)
2 cloves garlic, minced, or 1 teaspoon prepared minced garlic
5 ounces cremini or white mushrooms, finely chopped (3 cups)
3½ ounces fresh shiitake mushrooms, stemmed and finely chopped (1 cup)
1 teaspoon minced fresh thyme, or ¼ teaspoon dried thyme
2 teaspoons minced fresh chives
⅛ teaspoon salt

to make the pastry: Combine the flour, butter, nuts, and salt in a food processor; process, using a pulsing motion, until the mixture is crumbly. Add the egg and lemon juice; continue pulsing until the mixture begins to stick together. While the machine is running, add the water, 1 tablespoon at a time, just until the mixture forms a ball.

divide the pastry into 2 balls; wrap in plastic wrap or seal in plastic bags. Refrigerate for at least 1 hour or overnight.

meanwhile, make the duxelles: Melt 1 tablespoon of the butter in a large nonstick skillet over medium-high heat. Add the shallots and garlic; cook, stirring constantly, until the shallots are translucent, about 2 minutes. Melt the remaining 2 tablespoons butter in the pan; add the mushrooms and thyme. Reduce the heat to medium. Cook, stirring occasionally, until the liquid is completely evaporated and the mushrooms are tender, 8 to 10 minutes. Stir in the chives and salt. Taste and adjust the seasoning. Let cool.

to make the pinwheels: Preheat the oven to 375°F. Line a baking sheet with parchment paper. Place 1 ball of dough on a work surface covered with a sheet of waxed paper. Top with another sheet of waxed paper and press with the palm of your hand to flatten the ball. With a long side toward you, roll into an 8-by-10-inch rectangle. Repeat with the remaining pastry.

remove the waxed paper from 1 pastry sheet. Trim to even the edges. Spoon half of the mushroom mixture onto the center of the pastry; use a rubber spatula to spread it in an even and thin layer to the edges. Use both hands to lift the long edge of the pastry nearest you, then roll the pastry away from you, firmly and evenly. If time permits, wrap the pastry roll in plastic wrap and refrigerate for 30 minutes. (This will allow for easier cutting.) Using a serrated knife and a sawing motion, slice the roll into generous ¼-inch-thick slices.

place the slices, cut-side down, on the prepared baking sheet. Repeat with the remaining pastry. Bake the pinwheels, turning once, for 12 to 15 minutes, or until golden brown. Transfer to a wire rack to cool.

---

tip Shallots, a member of the onion family, are small bulbous herbs with a mild onion-garlic flavor. Always use fresh shallots; dehydrated ones have an inferior flavor. (If fresh are unavailable, substitute some onion and garlic.) Store shallots in a cool, dark place for up to 1 month; use before they begin to sprout. When sautéing, don't allow shallots to brown or they will taste bitter.

ADVANCE PREPARATION The uncut pastry will keep in the refrigerator in a tightly closed plastic bag for up to 2 days, or in the freezer for up to 2 months. If frozen, thaw overnight in the refrigerator before using. The duxelles will keep for up to 2 days in a covered container in the refrigerator. The completed pinwheels will keep for up to 2 days in a covered container in the refrigerator, or in the freezer for up to 1 month. If necessary, recrisp in a preheated 350°F oven for about 5 minutes before serving.

stuffed cheese puffs

MAKES ABOUT 24

Bake a batch of these puffs, using all three fillings.

- 4 tablespoons cold unsalted butter, cut into ½-inch pieces
- ½ cup freshly grated Parmesan cheese
- ½ cup unbleached all-purpose flour
- Dash of cayenne pepper (see Tip)
- Dash of salt

FILLING:

- 24 pimiento-stuffed green Spanish olives, drained and patted dry; or bottled cocktail onions, drained and patted dry; or halved dates rolled into balls; or any combination of these

combine the butter, Parmesan, flour, cayenne, and salt in a food processor; process until the mixture begins to come together. Remove and shape into a ball.

pinch off about 1 teaspoon of the dough, flatten slightly, wrap around an olive (or other filling), and roll the ball between your hands. Place on a baking sheet lined with parchment paper. Repeat with the remaining dough and fillings.

lightly cover the baking sheet with plastic wrap and refrigerate for about 1 hour.

preheat the oven to 350°F. Put the chilled baking sheet in the oven and bake the puffs for about 15 minutes, or until lightly browned.

serve warm, or transfer to a wire rack and serve at room temperature.

tip Cayenne pepper is the ground, dried pod of the cayenne chile. Use with caution, because it is very hot. Store in a tightly closed container in the refrigerator to retain its color and flavor.

ADVANCE PREPARATION The puffs can be rolled up to 1 day in advance; cover and refrigerate. Bake just before serving. The baked puffs can be made up to 2 days in advance; cover and refrigerate. Serve at room temperature or reheat in a preheated 350°F oven for about 5 minutes, or until heated through.

glazed pecans

MAKES 2 CUPS

Crunchy and slightly sweet, these make elegant snacks and are a must in Radicchio Cups Stuffed with Mesclun (page 74). Make an extra batch if you dare.

2 tablespoons unsalted butter
2 tablespoons light corn syrup
1 tablespoon water
½ teaspoon salt
2 cups (8 ounces) whole pecans (see Tip)

preheat the oven to 250°F. Line a jelly-roll pan with aluminum foil and spray it with vegetable-oil cooking spray.

melt the butter in a small nonstick saucepan over medium heat. Stir in the corn syrup, water, and salt. Bring to a boil.

remove the pan from the heat. Add the pecans and stir until completely coated.

spread the nuts on the prepared pan. Bake, stirring occasionally, for about 60 minutes, or until lightly browned and dry.

---

tip Because of their high fat content, nuts quickly become rancid at room temperature. Shelled nuts can be refrigerated in an airtight container for up to 4 months or frozen for up to 6 months. To freshen their flavor, spread the nuts on a baking sheet and heat in a preheated 150°F oven for a few minutes.

ADVANCE PREPARATION The nuts will keep for up to 3 weeks in an airtight container at room temperature.

spiced mixed nuts

MAKES 2½ CUPS

A holiday tradition that makes a party treat, a welcome gift, and for the busy cook, a sweet reward.

- ½ cup sugar
- 1 teaspoon ground cinnamon
- ½ teaspoon salt
- ¼ teaspoon ground nutmeg (see Tips)
- ¼ teaspoon ground allspice (see Tips)
- ¼ teaspoon ground ginger
- 1 egg white
- 2 tablespoons cold water
- 1 cup (4 ounces) whole walnuts
- ½ cup (2 ounces) unblanched almonds
- ½ cup (3 ounces) hazelnuts
- ½ cup (2 ounces) whole pecans

preheat the oven to 275°F. Line a jelly-roll pan with aluminum foil and spray it with vegetable-oil cooking spray.

combine the sugar, cinnamon, salt, nutmeg, allspice, and ginger in a medium bowl. Beat the egg white until foamy in a small bowl and stir in the water; stir into the sugar mixture. Add the nuts and stir until evenly coated.

using a slotted spoon, remove the nuts from the mixture, letting the excess sugar mixture drain off. Spread the nuts on the prepared pan. Bake, stirring occasionally, for about 45 minutes, or until lightly browned and dry. Let cool. When cool, break the nuts apart, if necessary.

tips Freshly grated nutmeg is more aromatic and flavorful than preground nutmeg. Use a nutmeg grater, which can be purchased in a kitchenware shop, to grate the entire nutmeg. Whole nutmeg will keep its flavor for years stored in a jar.

Spices such as nutmeg, allspice, cinnamon, and cumin are aromatic seasonings obtained from the seeds, flowers, stems, bark, or roots of various plants. Many are sold in both whole and ground forms. After grinding, spices quickly lose their aroma and flavor, so buy them in small quantities. Whole spices can be ground as needed. Store whole spices for up to 2 years in airtight containers in a cool, dark place.

ADVANCE PREPARATION The nuts will keep for up to 3 weeks in an airtight container at room temperature.

3

MEZZO BITES

Not too heavy, not too light. These plates can round out an appetizer party or augment a simple soup or salad to make an elegant and stylish meal.

Try Radicchio Cups Stuffed with Mesclun, Apples, and Glazed Pecans (page 74) as a first course at a sit-down dinner party. Roasted Vegetable Antipasto with Lemon-Caper Sauce (page 76) and Greek Green Beans and Tomatoes (page 70) are the answer to an appetizer buffet.

Big crowd? No problem. Double the recipes. (Plates are a must for these appetizers.)

crunchy szechuan green beans

MAKES 8 TO 12 SERVINGS (*vegan recipe*)

These green beans are so good you'll nibble them one by one. Adjust the amount of red pepper flakes or Chinese chili paste with garlic to suit your taste for heat.

- 1 tablespoon canola oil
- 1 pound green beans, trimmed
- ⅓ cup coarsely chopped onion
- ¼ cup hoisin sauce (see Tips)
- 2 tablespoons soy sauce
- 1 tablespoon Asian sesame oil
- 1 tablespoon water, or as needed
- 3 cloves garlic, minced, or 1½ teaspoons prepared minced garlic
- 1 teaspoon minced fresh ginger
- 1 teaspoon sugar
- ¼ teaspoon red pepper flakes, or 2 teaspoons Chinese chili paste with garlic (see Tips), or to taste
- Toasted sesame seeds (see Tip, page 50) for garnish

heat the canola oil in a large nonstick skillet over medium-high heat. Add the beans and onion; cook, stirring occasionally, until the beans are crisp-tender and blackened in spots, about 5 to 10 minutes, depending on their thickness.

meanwhile, whisk together all the remaining ingredients, except the sesame seeds, in a small bowl. Stir in more water as needed until the sauce has a cake-batter consistency. Set aside.

remove the beans from the heat. Add the sauce and stir until the beans are evenly coated. Taste and adjust the seasoning.

to serve, transfer the beans to a platter and garnish with sesame seeds. Serve warm or at room temperature. Use tongs for serving and provide plates and forks for your guests.

tips Hoisin sauce is a thick, sweet, reddish brown sauce made from soybeans, vinegar, chilies, spices, and garlic. It is sold in Asian markets and many supermarkets. Tightly sealed and refrigerated, it will keep almost indefinitely.

Chinese chili paste with garlic, sometimes labeled Chinese chili sauce or chili purée with garlic, is available in Asian markets and most supermarkets. Hot and spicy, it is made from chilies, rice vinegar, garlic, and salt, and is used in Szechuan cooking and as a condiment. After opening, store the tightly closed container in the refrigerator for up to 6 months.

ADVANCE PREPARATION The beans can be prepared up to 1 day in advance; cover and refrigerate. Bring to room temperature for serving.

greek green beans and tomatoes

MAKES 8 TO 12 SERVINGS *(vegan recipe)*

A traditional dish of Greek tavernas, served with platters of olives before the entrée. Accompany with Crostini (page 24) or Pita Crisps (page 23).

2 tablespoons olive oil
1 onion, thinly sliced (about 1½ cups)
4 cloves garlic, minced, or 2 teaspoons prepared minced garlic
1 pound green beans, trimmed
One 28-ounce can chopped tomatoes, with juice
2 tablespoons minced fresh flat-leaf parsley (see Tip)
Salt and freshly ground pepper to taste

heat the oil in a large nonstick sauté pan or skillet over medium heat. Add the onion and cook, stirring occasionally, until tender, about 6 minutes. Add the garlic and cook, stirring constantly until fragrant, about 1 minute. Stir in the beans, tomatoes and juice, and parsley.

when the liquid begins to simmer, reduce the heat to low; cover and cook until the beans are very tender, about 30 minutes. Remove the lid and continue to cook, stirring occasionally, until most of the liquid has evaporated. Add salt and pepper.

serve warm or at room temperature. Use tongs for serving and provide plates and forks for your guests.

tip Flat-leaf parsley, also called Italian parsley, has a more pungent flavor and is preferable to the more common curly-leaf parsley. Wash fresh parsley and shake off the excess moisture, then wrap the parsley in damp paper towels and store for up to 1 week in a plastic bag in the refrigerator. Avoid using dried parsley, which has little of fresh parsley's distinctive flavor.

ADVANCE PREPARATION The beans will keep for up to 4 days in a covered container in the refrigerator. Bring to room temperature before serving.

caesar crostini

MAKES 16

The noble Caesar never looked so good. If you're in a time crunch, you could use bottled Caesar dressing, but making the lemony mixture from scratch takes only minutes, using ingredients you probably have on hand.

16 Crostini (page 24), preferably made from a sourdough baguette
¼ cup freshly grated Parmesan cheese

CAESAR DRESSING:

2 tablespoons sour cream
1 tablespoon mayonnaise
1 tablespoon fresh lemon juice
1 tablespoon freshly grated Parmesan cheese
1 tablespoon minced fresh flat-leaf parsley
½ teaspoon Worcestershire sauce
1 clove garlic, minced, or ½ teaspoon prepared minced garlic
⅛ teaspoon Tabasco sauce, or to taste
⅛ teaspoon freshly ground pepper, or to taste
Salt to taste

TO COMPLETE THE RECIPE:

2½ cups finely shredded romaine hearts (see Tip, page 40)

preheat the oven to 350°F. Place the Crostini on a baking sheet and sprinkle with the Parmesan. Bake for about 3 minutes, or until the cheese is melted. Let cool.

to make the dressing: Whisk together all the dressing ingredients; in a medium bowl. Taste and adjust the seasoning (see Tip).

to serve, add the romaine lettuce to the dressing and toss. Using tongs, mound the lettuce on the Crostini. Provide plates for your guests.

---

tip To adjust the seasoning in a dressing, taste by dipping a salad ingredient, such as a lettuce leaf, into the dressing. Tasted from a spoon, most dressings will seem very strong.

VARIATION Mound the salad in Croustades (page 28).

ADVANCE PREPARATION The dressing will keep for up to 2 days in a covered container in the refrigerator. Assemble the appetizers just before serving.

apple salsa and brie crostini

MAKES 12 (2 CUPS SALSA)

Apples and cilantro are unpredictable partners in this zesty salsa, a sweet, cool, and crunchy complement to luscious Brie. Thank you to The 510, a Minneapolis restaurant where friends savored this appetizer at my birthday party. For a lighter bite, serve the salsa solo in endive leaves. Accompany with Crispy Tortilla Triangles (page 27) or Wonton Wedges (page 25).

APPLE SALSA:

2 tablespoons cider vinegar
1 teaspoon extra-virgin olive oil
½ teaspoon honey
Dash of salt and freshly ground pepper, or to taste
1 Granny Smith apple, peeled, cored, and finely diced (about 2 cups)
2 tablespoons finely chopped red bell pepper
2 tablespoons finely chopped red onion
2 tablespoons minced fresh cilantro (see Tip)

TO COMPLETE THE RECIPE:

12 Crostini (page 24)
½ cup rindless Brie cheese

preheat the broiler. To make the salsa: Stir together the vinegar, oil, honey, salt, and pepper in a medium bowl. Add the apple, bell pepper, onion, and cilantro; toss. Taste and adjust the seasoning.

to serve, mound each toast with 1 heaping tablespoon of the salsa. Top with about 2 teaspoons of the cheese. Arrange on a baking sheet. Broil 5 inches from the heat source for 1 minute, or until the cheese is melted. Serve warm.

tip Cilantro, also called Chinese parsley or fresh coriander, is commonly used for its distinctive pungent flavor and fragrance in Vietnamese, Thai, Chinese, Indian, and Mexican cuisines. Choose leaves with a bright, even color and no sign of wilting. The dried leaves lack fresh cilantro's distinctive flavor and are an unacceptable substitution.

VARIATION Substitute thinly sliced, white sandwich bread for the Crostini. Trim off the crusts and quarter the slices. Broil for about 1 minute on each side, or until crisp and lightly browned.

ADVANCE PREPARATION The salsa will keep for up to 2 days in a covered container in the refrigerator. Assemble and broil the appetizers just before serving.

radicchio cups stuffed with mesclun, apples, and glazed pecans

MAKES 6

This salad sings of autumn. Make the components ahead and assemble just before serving.

WALNUT VINAIGRETTE:

¼ cup walnut oil (see Tips)
2 tablespoons red wine vinegar
1 tablespoon fresh lemon juice
1 tablespoon minced shallot
2 teaspoons pure maple syrup
⅛ teaspoon freshly ground pepper, or to taste
⅛ teaspoon salt, or to taste

SALAD:

6 cups mixed baby greens (see Tips)
½ cup diced apple or pear
6 radicchio leaves (see Tips)
½ cup finely crumbled blue cheese
18 Glazed Pecans (page 65) or toasted walnuts (see Tip, page 58)

to make the vinaigrette: Whisk together all the dressing ingredients in a large bowl. Taste and adjust the seasoning.

add the greens to the vinaigrette and toss. Add the apple or pear and toss again.

to serve, use tongs to transfer the mixture to the radicchio leaves. Sprinkle with the cheese and top each serving with 3 pecans. Serve immediately. Provide plates and forks for your guests.

---

tips Walnut oil has a pleasant, nutty taste and is used mainly for salads, rather than as a cooking medium. Because it turns rancid quickly, refrigerate after opening. It will keep for up to 3 months. For the best flavor, buy roasted-walnut oil made from roasted walnuts.

Mixed baby greens, also called mesclun, come in a prewashed mix that usually includes arugula, frisée, mizuma, oak leaf lettuce, and radicchio leaves. If refrigerated in a plastic bag, they will last for up to 5 days.

Radicchio is a red-leafed Italian chicory. The most common variety has burgundy-red leaves with white ribs that grow to form a small, round loose head. The leaves are tender but firm, with a slightly bitter flavor. Store radicchio for up to 1 week in a plastic bag in the refrigerator.

roasted vegetable antipasto with lemon-caper sauce

MAKES ABOUT 8 SERVINGS (½ CUP SAUCE)

This stunning dish of glistening vegetables looks great on the buffet table. Immediately after roasting, arrange the hot vegetables on a platter. Add olives and marinated artichoke hearts, if you like. Serve the sauce in a bowl with a basket of Crostini (page 24), and provide plates and forks. Or chop the roasted vegetables to serve in Croustades (page 28) and drizzle with the sauce.

ROASTED VEGETABLES:

¼ cup olive oil
4 cloves garlic, minced, or 2 teaspoons prepared minced garlic
1 teaspoon minced fresh oregano
1 teaspoon minced fresh rosemary
1 teaspoon minced fresh thyme
¼ teaspoon freshly ground pepper
Pinch of salt
8 medium-thick asparagus spears, trimmed
½ eggplant, peeled and cut into ½-inch-thick wedges
2 portobello mushrooms, stemmed and cut into ½-inch-wide strips
1 red bell pepper, seeded, deribbed, and cut lengthwise into 1-inch-wide strips
1 zucchini, halved horizontally, and cut into ½-inch-thick wedges
½ red onion, cut into ½-inch-thick wedges

LEMON-CAPER SAUCE:

¼ cup mayonnaise
2 tablespoons fresh lemon juice
1 teaspoon Dijon mustard
½ teaspoon honey
1 clove garlic, minced, or 1 teaspoon prepared minced garlic
1 teaspoon minced shallot
1 teaspoon capers, drained and rinsed
1 teaspoon minced fresh thyme, or ½ teaspoon dried thyme
⅛ teaspoon freshly ground pepper, or to taste
Salt to taste

TO COMPLETE THE RECIPE:

Coarsely crumbled feta or shredded Parmesan cheese, toasted pine nuts (see Tip, page 16), and fresh basil sprigs for garnish

continued »

to prepare the roasted vegetables: Preheat the oven to 425°F. Line a large jelly-roll pan (see Tip) with aluminum foil.

stir together the oil, garlic, oregano, rosemary, thyme, pepper, and salt in a large bowl. Add all the vegetables and toss to coat.

spread the vegetables in a single layer on the prepared pan. Bake, turning the vegetables occasionally, for 15 to 20 minutes, or until crisp-tender and lightly browned.

to make the sauce: While the vegetables are roasting, stir together all the sauce ingredients in a small bowl. Taste and adjust the seasoning.

to serve, transfer the vegetables to a serving platter. Garnish with cheese, nuts, and basil sprigs. Serve warm or at room temperature. Serve the room-temperature sauce in a bowl on the side; provide a small spoon for drizzling over individual servings of vegetables.

tip A jelly-roll pan is a rectangular baking pan with sides about 1 inch high. It can be used for baking sheet cakes but is also ideal for broiling, toasting nuts and seeds, and baking any mixture that might run over the edges of a nonsided baking sheet.

VARIATION For a vegan appetizer, substitute Roasted Red Bell Pepper Sauce (page 22) for the Lemon-Caper Sauce.

ADVANCE PREPARATION The sauce will keep for up to 2 days in a covered container in the refrigerator. The vegetables can be roasted up to 1 day in advance; cover and refrigerate. Bring to room temperature before serving.

mushroom caps with basil-pecan stuffing

MAKES 6

A foolproof recipe, and a crowd-pleaser when doubled. Use large mushrooms and plan for just one per guest if other appetizers are also served. The stuffing works equally well in smaller caps.

6 large (about 2½ inches in diameter) white mushrooms (see Tip)
Olive oil for brushing

BASIL-PECAN STUFFING:

1 tablespoon unsalted butter
½ cup finely chopped onion
2 cloves garlic, minced, or 1 teaspoon prepared minced garlic
¼ cup toasted wheat germ
2 tablespoons finely chopped pecans
2 tablespoons freshly grated Parmesan cheese
1 tablespoon soy sauce
1 tablespoon minced fresh flat-leaf parsley
1 tablespoon minced fresh basil
Freshly ground pepper to taste

TO COMPLETE THE RECIPE:

Dash of sweet Hungarian paprika, or to taste

preheat the oven to 375°F. Remove the stems from the mushrooms. Finely chop enough stems to yield ½ cup and set aside (discard the rest). Lightly brush the mushroom caps with oil. Place the caps, rounded-side down, on a baking sheet lined with parchment paper. Set aside.

to make the stuffing: Melt the butter in a medium nonstick skillet over medium-high heat. Add the onion and cook, stirring occasionally, until fragrant, about 1 minute. Add the mushroom stems and garlic; continue cooking, stirring occasionally, until the mushrooms and onion are tender, about 4 minutes.

remove the pan from the heat. Stir in all the remaining stuffing ingredients. Taste and adjust the seasoning.

to serve, fill the mushroom caps with the stuffing; sprinkle with paprika. Bake for about 10 minutes, or until the stuffing is heated through and lightly browned. Serve immediately.

continued »

tip Refrigerate mushrooms for up to 4 days in a paper bag, an open plastic bag, or a basket so air can circulate around them. Do not clean prior to storage; before using, simply brush with a mushroom brush or wipe with a moist paper towel. If it is necessary to rinse them, do so quickly; because mushrooms are very absorbent, they should not be allowed to soak in water. Before using, cut any woody ends from the bottoms of the tender stems. Mushrooms should be cooked quickly; they are 90 percent water, and overcooking results in a mushy texture.

ADVANCE PREPARATION The stuffing can be made up to 1 day in advance; cover and refrigerate. The mushrooms can be stuffed up to 2 hours before baking; cover and refrigerate. Bring to room temperature before baking.

mixed mushroom-almond pâté

MAKES 1½ CUPS *(vegan recipe)*

Not just any pâté, this one is rich-tasting yet light, and is made with full-flavored wild mushrooms. The smooth texture spreads nicely on Bagel Chips (page 26), and it's delicious on Pita Crisps (page 23), Crostini (page 24), wedges of pita bread (preferably Lebanese pita bread with no pocket), or thick slices of crusty baguettes. Serve cornichons (see Tips) on the side.

- 1 tablespoon olive oil
- 5 ounces cremini mushrooms, sliced (1 cup); see Tips
- 3 ounces oyster mushrooms, stemmed and sliced (½ cup); see Tips
- 3 ounces shiitake mushrooms, stemmed and sliced (½ cup); see Tips
- ½ cup coarsely chopped onion
- 2 cloves garlic, minced, or 1 teaspoon prepared minced garlic
- 2 teaspoons minced fresh tarragon, or ½ teaspoon dried tarragon
- 1 cup (4½ ounces) slivered almonds
- 1 tablespoon fresh lemon juice
- 1 tablespoon soy sauce
- Ground white pepper to taste

TO COMPLETE THE RECIPE:

- Fresh flat-leaf parsley sprigs, red bell pepper strips, or slivered almonds for garnish

heat the oil in a large nonstick skillet over medium-high heat. Add the mushrooms, onion, and garlic; cook, stirring occasionally, until the mushrooms are tender, about 5 minutes. Remove from the heat, stir in the tarragon, and let cool.

transfer the mushroom mixture to a food processor (or blender). Add all the remaining ingredients, except the garnish, and process until smooth. Taste and adjust the seasoning.

transfer the pâté to a bowl. Let stand for at least 1 hour before serving. Garnish with parsley, bell pepper, or almonds and serve at room temperature.

tips Cremini mushrooms (sometimes labeled "Italian brown mushrooms") are more flavorful and have a denser, less watery texture than white mushrooms. Portobello mushrooms are larger, matured cremini.

Oyster mushrooms are graceful, fluted mushrooms that vary in color from pale gray to dark brownish gray. Their seafoodlike flavor is robust and slightly peppery but becomes much milder when cooked. Look for young mushrooms, 1½ inches or less in diameter; remove the stems before cooking.

Fresh shiitakes are large, umbrella-shaped mushrooms, brown-black in color, with a rich and unique flavor. Choose plump mushrooms with edges that turn under; avoid broken or shriveled caps. Store shiitake mushrooms in the refrigerator for up to 3 days, in a dish covered with a damp cloth or paper towel rather than in a closed container or plastic bag. The stems are extremely tough and should be removed. You can use them to add flavor to stocks and sauces; discard the stems after they have been used for flavoring.

Cornichons are crisp, tart French pickles made from tiny gherkin cucumbers.

ADVANCE PREPARATION The pâté will keep for up to 1 week in a covered container in the refrigerator. Bring to room temperature before serving.

oregano egg salad on pumpernickel toast

MAKES 16

This extravagant egg salad, laced with oregano and olives, is anything but ordinary, especially on dark pumpernickel toast. Or, serve it with Bagel Chips (page 26), Pita Crisps (page 23), Crostini (page 24), or Toast Points (page 29).

DRESSING:

2 tablespoons mayonnaise
1 teaspoon Dijon mustard
1 teaspoon fresh lemon juice
1 teaspoon minced fresh oregano, or ¼ teaspoon dried oregano
1 clove garlic, minced, or ½ teaspoon prepared minced garlic
Salt and freshly ground pepper to taste

SALAD:

3 hard-cooked eggs (see Tip)
2 tablespoons finely chopped carrot
2 tablespoons coarsely chopped kalamata olives
1 tablespoon finely chopped red bell pepper
1 tablespoon finely chopped red onion

TO COMPLETE THE RECIPE:

16 slices thinly sliced party pumpernickel bread (about 2¼ inches square)
Tiny fresh oregano sprigs for garnish

preheat the oven to 400°F. To make the dressing: Whisk together all the dressing ingredients in a small bowl.

mash the eggs with a fork in a medium bowl. Stir in the carrot, olives, bell pepper, and onion. Add the dressing and stir again. Taste and adjust the seasoning.

arrange the bread slices on a baking sheet. Toast in the oven for about 2 minutes on each side, or until crusty but not firm all the way through. Transfer to wire racks to cool.

to serve, top each toast with about 1½ tablespoons of the egg salad and garnish with oregano sprigs.

tip To hard-cook eggs, put them in a single layer in a saucepan and cover with at least 1 inch of cold water. Cover and bring the water to a full rolling boil over medium-high heat. Remove the pan from the heat and let the eggs stand in the water, covered, for about 15 minutes for large eggs. (For larger or smaller eggs, adjust the time up or down by about 3 minutes for each size variation.) Drain off the hot water and immediately cover the eggs with cold water; let stand until the eggs are completely cool, then drain. (This cooling process prevents a dark gray-green surface from forming around the yolk. If it does occur, the greenish color is harmless and does not alter the nutritional value or flavor of the egg. Quick cooling also causes the eggs to contract, making them easier to peel.) Refrigerate hard-cooked eggs for up to 1 week.

ADVANCE PREPARATION The egg salad will keep for up to 2 days in a covered container in the refrigerator. Assemble with the bread just before serving.

curried roasted potato wedges with sour cream–chive dip

MAKES 32 (3/4 CUP DIP)

Curry heats this robust classic. Prepare the potatoes for roasting up to 1 hour in advance, then roast them just before serving and let them fill your kitchen with enticing aromas.

- 2 large Yukon Gold or russet potatoes, scrubbed but not peeled (see Tip)
- 2 tablespoons canola oil
- 2 teaspoons curry powder

SOUR CREAM-CHIVE DIP:

- ¾ cup sour cream
- 2 tablespoons minced fresh chives
- 1 tablespoon fresh lemon juice
- 1 clove garlic, minced, or ½ teaspoon prepared minced garlic
- ¼ teaspoon salt, plus more to taste

preheat the oven to 400°F. Cut each potato in half lengthwise, then cut each half lengthwise into 8 wedges. Combine the oil and curry powder in a medium bowl. Add the potatoes and toss until evenly coated.

arrange the potatoes in a single layer on a jelly-roll pan. Roast for about 25 to 30 minutes, turning once, or until golden brown on all sides and tender when tested with a fork.

meanwhile, make the dip: Stir together all the dip ingredients in a small bowl. Taste and adjust the seasoning. Set aside.

to serve, use a slotted spatula to transfer the potato wedges to a plate lined with a paper towel; pat gently. Transfer to a serving dish and sprinkle lightly with salt. Serve warm, with a bowl of dip on the side.

tip Store potatoes in a cool, dry, well-ventilated, dark place for 1 to 2 weeks. Do not store in the refrigerator; their starch will convert to sugar, and they may turn brown when cooked. If stored in bright light, potatoes will turn green and develop a bitter flavor.

ADVANCE PREPARATION The dip will keep for up to 3 days in a covered container in the refrigerator. Bring to room temperature before serving with freshly roasted potatoes.

SIZABLE BITES

Big bold flavors on little plates, these hearty appetizers can anchor an appetizer buffet or serve as a side dish to a light entrée. Bright, generous in size, savory, and drizzled with sauces, they require plates and forks.

Pair Fresh Spring Rolls with Spicy Peanut Sauce (page 113) and Five-Spice Diced Vegetables in Endive Leaves with Plum Sauce (page 94) for an Asian theme. Or, choose Savory Nut Balls with Zesty Tomato Sauce (page 105) and Caramelized-Onion Frittata with Chimichurri Sauce (page 120) for a hearty selection.

The edible containers, which include filo cups, potato cups, and endive leaves, and the foundations, which include wonton wraps, egg roll wraps, pitas, and tortillas, offer texture, variety, and good taste.

tomato-basil bruschetta

MAKES 8

Every Italian trattoria offers its version of bruschetta made with the best tomatoes I have ever tasted. To serve these open-faced sandwiches warm, sprinkle them with Parmesan cheese and broil just before serving. For room-temperature presentation, omit the Parmesan and spread a thin layer of fresh, white goat cheese or Boursin cheese (see Tips) over the bread before adding the tomato mixture. The cheese will prevent the bread from becoming soggy, allowing you to prepare these in advance.

Eight ½- to ¾-inch-thick slices fresh or day-old French or Italian bread

TOMATO-BASIL TOPPING:

2 tomatoes, coarsely chopped (about 2 cups); see Tips
¼ cup minced fresh basil
1 tablespoon extra-virgin olive oil
2 cloves garlic, minced, or 1 teaspoon prepared minced garlic
Salt and freshly ground pepper to taste

TO COMPLETE THE RECIPE:

2 tablespoons freshly grated Parmesan cheese

preheat the broiler or a dry stovetop grill pan, preheat the oven to 400°F, or prepare a charcoal fire (the traditional method). Or, use a toaster oven or a toaster that accommodates wide slices of bread.

toast or grill the bread slices on both sides until they are golden brown and crisp on the outside, yet still chewy and not dry on the inside. If you are using the broiler or oven, arrange the bread slices in a single layer on a baking sheet. Toast the bread slices in the oven for about 3 minutes on each side. The time will be less under a broiler, over a charcoal fire, or on a dry stovetop grill pan. Watch closely so the bread does not burn.

to make the topping: Stir together all the topping ingredients in a small bowl. Taste and adjust the seasoning.

continued ››

to serve, preheat the broiler. Place the bruschetta in a single layer on a baking sheet. Top with the tomato mixture; sprinkle with the Parmesan. Broil 4 to 5 inches from the heating element for about 2 minutes, or until the cheese is melted. Serve immediately.

tips Boursin cheese is a white cheese with a buttery texture. It is available flavored with herbs, garlic, or coarsely cracked pepper.

Because cool temperatures reduce the flavor of tomatoes and can make their texture mealy, do not store them in the refrigerator. Instead, store them at room temperature. Tomatoes will become redder, softer, juicier, and tastier as they ripen. Once they are fully ripened, use within 2 days.

VARIATION While warm, rub one side of each bread slice with a cut garlic clove; the more you rub, the stronger the flavor. Or, spread the warm toasts with Roasted Garlic (page 20). Then add the topping.

ADVANCE PREPARATION The topping will keep for up to 1 day in a covered container in the refrigerator. Bring the topping to room temperature; assemble and broil the bruschetta just before serving.

cumin-scented potatoes in filo cups

MAKES 12

A much-requested recipe from an East Indian friend, Raghavan Iyer. The filo cups are easy to make, but you can also use frozen, mini filo-dough shells, available in most supermarkets. They are smaller and accommodate about 1 heaping tablespoon of filling, so the recipe would yield about 64 mezzo bites.

FILO CUPS:

4 sheets frozen filo dough, thawed (see Tips)
2 tablespoons unsalted butter, melted

FILLING:

1 pound red-skinned potatoes (see Tips), scrubbed but not peeled
Dash of salt, plus more to taste
2 tablespoons canola oil
1 teaspoon whole cumin seeds
¼ cup finely chopped onion
2 teaspoons curry powder, or to taste
1 cup frozen baby peas
¼ cup minced fresh cilantro

to make the filo cups: Preheat the oven to 350°F. Place 1 filo sheet on a cutting board; lightly brush with butter. Top with the remaining sheets, stacking one at a time and lightly brushing each with butter. Cut the stacked sheets into 12 squares. Mold the squares into muffin cups, allowing the pointed ends to extend above the cups. Bake for 4 to 6 minutes, or until golden brown. Let cool in the pans on a wire rack.

to make the filling: Put the potatoes in a large saucepan and cover with water. Bring the water to a boil over high heat; stir in a dash of salt. Reduce the heat to medium-high and cook until the potatoes are tender when pierced with a fork, about 10 to 15 minutes. Be careful not to overcook. Drain well and rinse with cold water. When the potatoes are cool enough to handle, peel and cut into ¼-inch dice. Set aside.

continued »

heat the oil in a large nonstick skillet over medium heat. Add the cumin seeds; stir constantly for about 30 seconds, or until lightly browned and aromatic. Add the onion and curry powder; cook, stirring constantly, until the onion is golden brown, about 3 minutes. Add the potatoes and all the remaining ingredients; stir until the potatoes are evenly coated with curry powder. Taste and adjust the seasoning.

to serve warm, spoon about ¼ cup of the filling into each filo cup; serve immediately. Or, let the filling come to room temperature before spooning into the cups. Provide plates for your guests.

tips Filo (also spelled phyllo and fillo) is a tissue-thin pastry that is sold in the freezer section of most supermarkets. Thaw frozen filo overnight, or for at least 12 hours, in the refrigerator; it becomes brittle if refrozen. It also becomes dry and brittle when exposed to the air, so do not unwrap the sheets until all the other recipe ingredients and equipment are ready. Use plastic wrap topped by a slightly damp cloth to cover the sheets as you use them. The filo sheets from the interior of a package are often sturdier than those at the beginning or end of the stack. However, don't worry if some of the sheets have a few tears; the layering will camouflage any imperfections.

Red potatoes are thin-skinned and sweet. They are also low in starch, which prevents them from breaking apart easily after cooking. Do not refrigerate; instead, store them for up to 2 weeks at room temperature in a cool, dark place.

VARIATION For a vegan appetizer, brush the filo dough with canola oil instead of butter.

ADVANCE PREPARATION The filo cups can be made up to 1 day in advance. Do not remove from the pans. Lightly cover the pans with plastic wrap and store at room temperature. The potato filling will keep for up to 2 days in a covered container in the refrigerator. Bring to room temperature before serving.

five-spice diced vegetables in endive leaves with plum sauce

MAKES 20 (*vegan recipe*)

The licorice tones of Chinese five-spice powder give this appetizer character. Vary the vegetables to include your favorites or to use up odds and ends. (You'll need a total of about 4 cups of diced vegetables.) For larger servings, fill 6 baby romaine or radicchio leaves or Filo Cups (page 91) with heaping quarter-cupfuls of the vegetables.

PLUM SAUCE:

- ¼ cup bottled Chinese plum sauce
- 1 tablespoon water, or as needed

FIVE-SPICE DICED VEGETABLES:

- 3 ribs bok choy
- 20 endive leaves, ends trimmed
- 1 tablespoon fresh lime juice
- 2 tablespoons soy sauce
- 1 tablespoon minced fresh cilantro, or 2 teaspoons minced fresh mint, or to taste
- ½ teaspoon Chinese five-spice powder (see Tips)
- ⅛ teaspoon red pepper flakes, or to taste
- Ground white pepper to taste
- 1 tablespoon roasted-peanut oil (see Tips) or canola oil
- 2 carrots, cut into ¼-inch dice (about 1 cup)
- ½ cup diced red bell pepper
- ¼ cup diced yellow bell pepper
- 2 green onions (white and green parts), finely chopped
- 2 cloves garlic, minced, or 1 teaspoon prepared minced garlic

TO COMPLETE THE RECIPE:

- Toasted sesame seeds (see Tip, page 50) for garnish

to make the sauce: Pour the bottled plum sauce into a small bowl. Stir in water as needed until the sauce is a maple-syrup consistency. Set aside.

cut the green tops of the bok choy ribs into fine shreds (see Tip, page 40); cut the white ribs into ½-inch dice. Set aside.

arrange the endive leaves on a platter. Stir together the lime juice, soy sauce, cilantro or mint, five-spice powder, red pepper flakes, and white pepper in a small bowl. Set aside.

continued »

heat the oil in a large nonstick skillet over medium-high heat. Add the bok choy, carrots, bell peppers, green onions, and garlic. Cook, stirring constantly, until crisp-tender, about 4 to 5 minutes. Remove from the heat; stir in the lime juice mixture. Taste and adjust the seasoning.

serve the vegetables warm or let them come to room temperature. Fill each endive leaf with a heaping tablespoon of the vegetable mixture, drizzle with about 1 teaspoon of the plum sauce, and sprinkle with sesame seeds. Provide plates for your guests.

tips Five-spice powder, sometimes called five-fragrance powder, is a sweet and pungent mixture of ground fennel, star anise, ginger, licorice root, cinnamon, and cloves. A licorice flavor predominates. It is available in Asian markets and most supermarkets.

Roasted-peanut oil, available in many supermarkets, is more aromatic and flavorful than other peanut oils because it is made from peanuts that are dry-roasted prior to pressing.

ADVANCE PREPARATION The vegetables can be chopped up to 1 day in advance; put in zip-top plastic bags and refrigerate. Cook the vegetables just before serving.

herbed diced vegetables in crisp new potato cups

MAKES 16 *(vegan recipe)*

Pretty, little potato cups are stuffed with diced vegetables and herbs. Try them filled with the warm Roasted Red Pepper and Feta Stuffing (page 52) or at room temperature with layers of crumbled hard-cooked egg (see Tip, page 85), crème fraîche, and Black-Olive Caviar (page 32).

CRISP NEW POTATO CUPS:

8 new potatoes (see Tip, page 93), scrubbed but not peeled, halved crosswise
Olive oil for brushing

HERBED DICED VEGETABLES:

1 tablespoon olive oil
¼ cup finely chopped onion
2 cloves garlic, minced, or 1 teaspoon prepared minced garlic
½ cup finely diced carrot
½ cup tiny cauliflower florets
½ cup tiny broccoli florets and finely chopped tender stems
2 tablespoons minced fresh flat-leaf parsley
2 tablespoons toasted wheat germ (see Tip) or dried bread crumbs
1 tablespoon soy sauce
1 teaspoon minced fresh thyme, or ¼ teaspoon dried thyme
1 teaspoon minced fresh marjoram, or ¼ teaspoon dried marjoram
Salt and freshly ground pepper to taste

to make the cups: Preheat the broiler. Line a baking sheet with aluminum foil. Using a sharp knife, even the bottoms of the potatoes so that the halves will stand on end. Using a melon baller, scoop out the potato flesh, leaving a ⅛- to ¼-inch-thick shell. Lightly brush all surfaces of the potato cups with oil. Place the cups, scooped-side up, on the prepared baking sheet. Broil for about 8 minutes, or until tender and lightly browned. Use tongs to transfer the cups, scooped-side down, to a plate lined with a paper towel and let drain. Cover to keep warm.

continued »

while the cups are broiling, make the vegetables: Heat the oil in a medium nonstick skillet over medium-high heat. Add the onion and garlic; cook, stirring constantly until the onion is translucent, about 3 minutes. Add the carrot, cauliflower, and broccoli; continue cooking, stirring constantly, until tender, about 4 minutes. Remove the pan from the heat. Stir in all the remaining filling ingredients. Taste and adjust the seasoning.

to serve, spoon about 1 heaping teaspoon of the vegetable mixture into each potato cup. Serve immediately.

tip Wheat germ, the embryo of the wheat berry, is rich in vitamins, minerals, and protein. Toasted wheat germ, found in the cereal aisle of most supermarkets, is preferable to raw wheat germ in most recipes because of its nutty flavor and slightly crunchy texture. To prevent rancidity, store toasted wheat germ for up to 6 months in a tightly closed container in the refrigerator.

VARIATION Serve the Herbed Diced Vegetables in Croustades (page 28) or Filo Cups (page 91) instead of the potato cups.

ADVANCE PREPARATION The potato cups and filling can be made early in the day; cover and refrigerate separately. Reheat the cups in a preheated 350°F oven for about 5 minutes, or until heated through. Reheat the filling in a dry skillet over low heat. Fill the cups just before serving.

wontons with herbed tomato sauce

MAKES 24 (⅓ CUP SAUCE)

Inspired by the flavors of my favorite lasagna, these wontons are as easy as they are smart. Also try them with Roasted Red Bell Pepper Sauce (page 22).

HERBED TOMATO SAUCE:

¼ cup tomato paste (see Tip)
2 tablespoons water
2 tablespoons extra-virgin olive oil
2 tablespoons red wine vinegar
2 cloves garlic, minced, or 1 teaspoon prepared minced garlic
1 tablespoon minced fresh basil, or ½ teaspoon dried basil
2 teaspoons minced fresh oregano, or ½ teaspoon dried oregano
½ teaspoon freshly ground pepper, or to taste
Salt to taste

FILLING:

½ cup ricotta cheese
½ cup coarsely shredded Monterey Jack cheese
½ cup frozen chopped spinach, thawed and squeezed dry
2 tablespoons toasted pine nuts (see Tip, page 16)
1 tablespoon minced fresh basil, or ½ teaspoon dried basil
1 teaspoon minced fresh oregano, or ¼ teaspoon dried oregano
1 teaspoon fresh lemon juice
1 clove garlic, minced, or ½ teaspoon prepared minced garlic
Pinch of red pepper flakes, or to taste
¼ teaspoon freshly ground pepper, or to taste
Salt to taste

TO COMPLETE THE RECIPE:

24 square wonton skins
About 1 tablespoon olive oil, or as needed

preheat the oven to 375°F. Line a baking sheet with baking parchment paper or aluminum foil.

to make the sauce: Stir together all the sauce ingredients in a small bowl. Taste and adjust the seasoning. Let stand at room temperature for about 20 minutes to allow the flavors to blend.

to make the filling: Stir together all the filling ingredients in a medium bowl. Taste and adjust the seasoning.

spoon about ½ tablespoon of the filling into the center of a wonton skin. Lightly brush the edges (about ¼ to ½ inch) of the skin with water. Bring the 4 corners of the skin together to cover the filling; pinch to seal. Place the wonton on the baking sheet. Lightly brush the top and sides of the wonton with the oil. Repeat with the remaining filling and skins.

to serve, bake the wontons for 12 to 15 minutes, or until golden brown. Arrange the warm wontons on a plate with a bowl of sauce on the side for dipping. Provide plates for your guests.

---

tip Concentrated tomato paste is available in tubes, ideal for recipes calling for less than a 6-ounce can. Refrigerate the tube after opening.

ADVANCE PREPARATION The sauce will keep for up to 3 days in a covered container in the refrigerator. Bring to room temperature before serving. The wontons can be assembled early in the day; cover and refrigerate. Bring to room temperature, then brush with oil and bake just before serving. Or, bake them, then cover and refrigerate; microwave on high for about 1 minute before serving.

samosas with mango chutney

MAKES 30

With packaged spring roll wrappers, these spicy samosas are a snap. Many thanks to my friend Nathan Fong, an award-winning Chinese-Canadian food stylist, for this recipe.

FILLING:

3 potatoes, peeled and cut into 2-inch-thick slices
1 tablespoon canola oil
¼ cup finely chopped onion
4 cloves garlic, minced, or 2 teaspoons prepared minced garlic
1 tablespoon minced jalapeño chile
1 teaspoon minced fresh ginger
1 teaspoon ground coriander
1 teaspoon ground cumin
½ cup frozen baby peas
⅓ cup frozen corn kernels
2 green onions (white and green parts), finely chopped
2 tablespoons coarsely chopped fresh cilantro
1 tablespoon fresh lemon juice
½ teaspoon garam masala (see Tips)
Salt and freshly ground pepper to taste

TO COMPLETE THE RECIPE:

Ten 7- to 8-inch square spring roll wrappers (see Tips)
Canola oil for cooking
About ⅓ cup prepared mango chutney

to make the filling: Bring a medium pot of salted water to a boil over high heat. Add the potato slices; when the water returns to a boil, reduce the heat to medium. Cover and cook until tender, about 10 minutes; drain well.

meanwhile, heat the oil in a large nonstick skillet over medium-high heat. Add the onion and garlic; cook, stirring constantly, until the onion is translucent, about 2 minutes. Add the chile, ginger, coriander, and cumin; cook, stirring constantly, for about 1 minute. Stir in all the remaining filling ingredients except the potatoes. Remove from the heat.

coarsely mash the potatoes; add to the skillet. Stir until the mixture is evenly combined. Taste and adjust the seasoning. Set aside to cool.

continued ››

cut the spring roll wrappers into thirds to form strips. Spoon 1 tablespoon of the filling mixture onto one end of a strip and diagonally fold the strip over the filling to form a triangle. Continue folding, alternating to the left and right, maintaining the triangle shape. When a square of pastry remains at the end, lightly brush it with water. Continue folding and press the end to seal.

pour oil to a depth of about ½ inch into a large sauté pan or skillet. Heat over medium-high heat until a drop of water sizzles when added. Reduce the heat to medium and add the samosas. Cook for about 2 minutes on each side, or until lightly browned. Use a slotted spoon to transfer the samosas to a plate lined with paper towels; pat gently.

to serve, transfer the samosas to a platter and serve hot with a bowl of chutney on the side for dipping. Provide plates for your guests.

tips *Garam* is the Indian word for a sensation of warmth felt while eating, and *masala* means blend. Garam masala, the blend of dry-roasted ground spices from northern India, is not hot-tasting, but it is meant to generate a feeling of warmth. The spice blend can be purchased in Indian markets and in the ethnic section of some supermarkets.

Spring roll wrappers, also known as egg roll skins, are thin square or round sheets of dough made from flour, eggs, and salt. Traditionally, they are used to make wontons and egg rolls. Purchase them in the refrigerator or freezer section in Asian markets and in some supermarkets.

ADVANCE PREPARATION The filling can be made up to 1 day in advance; cover and refrigerate. The assembled but uncooked samosas can be tightly wrapped and frozen for up to 1 month. Cook while frozen.

savory nut balls with zesty tomato sauce

MAKES 16 (¼ CUP SAUCE)

Your nonvegetarian friends won't say "Where's the beef?" when they taste these savory bites, as substantial and satisfying as meatballs.

ZESTY TOMATO SAUCE:

¼ cup tomato paste
2 tablespoons water
⅛ teaspoon red pepper flakes, or to taste (see Tip)
⅛ teaspoon ground coriander
⅛ teaspoon ground cumin
⅛ teaspoon freshly ground pepper, or to taste

NUT BALLS:

½ cup finely chopped walnuts
½ cup dried bread crumbs
2 tablespoons toasted sesame seeds (see Tip, page 50)
1 tablespoon finely chopped onion
1 tablespoon minced fresh flat-leaf parsley
1 tablespoon soy sauce
2 cloves garlic, minced, or 1 teaspoon prepared minced garlic
1 teaspoon minced fresh thyme, or ¼ teaspoon dried thyme
1 egg, lightly beaten
1 tablespoon canola oil

to make the sauce: Stir together all the sauce ingredients in a small bowl. Let stand at room temperature to allow the flavors to blend. Taste and adjust the seasoning.

to make the nut balls: Stir together all the nut ball ingredients, except the egg and oil, in a medium bowl. Add the egg. To form each ball, roll about 1 tablespoon of the mixture between your hands, pressing gently and firmly as you roll.

heat the oil in a large nonstick skillet over medium-high heat; add the nut balls. Cook, rolling and turning occasionally, until lightly browned and firm, about 5 minutes. Transfer the nut balls to a plate lined with a paper towel; pat gently.

continued »

to serve, transfer the warm nut balls to a platter; provide a container of cocktail picks. Serve the sauce in a small bowl on the side for dipping.

tip Red pepper flakes, also called crushed red pepper, are the seeds and flakes of fiery hot peppers; a small amount goes a long way! Refrigerate in a tightly covered container to preserve the color and flavor.

VARIATIONS Substitute Roasted Red Bell Pepper Sauce (page 22), Herbed Tomato Sauce (page 100), Creamy Horseradish Sauce (page 116), or Chimichurri Sauce (page 120) for the Zesty Tomato Sauce.

For the Nut Balls, replace ¼ cup of the finely chopped walnuts with ¼ cup finely chopped hazelnuts.

ADVANCE PREPARATION The sauce will keep for up to 3 days in a covered container in the refrigerator; bring to room temperature for serving. The nut ball mixture will keep for up to 1 day in a covered container in the refrigerator; sauté the nut balls just before serving. Or, cook the nut balls, cover, and refrigerate; reheat in a preheated 350°F oven for about 5 minutes.

yam croquettes with tangerine-sherry sauce

MAKES 16 (⅓ CUP SAUCE)

Made with sweet, colorful yams, these croquettes are veggie mini-burgers. If tangerines aren't available, try them with Chimichurri Sauce (page 120), Roasted Red Bell Pepper Sauce (page 22), or topped with a dollop of sour cream, a cherry tomato half, and a tiny sprig of fresh flat-leaf parsley.

TANGERINE-SHERRY SAUCE:

2 tablespoons mayonnaise
2 tablespoons fresh tangerine juice
2 teaspoons extra-virgin olive oil
2 teaspoons dry sherry (see Tips)
1 teaspoon minced jalapeño chile, or to taste
Salt to taste

YAM CROQUETTES:

2 tablespoons olive oil, divided
1 cup coarsely shredded peeled yam (see Tips)
½ cup finely chopped red onion
½ cup finely chopped celery
2 cloves garlic, minced, or 1 teaspoon prepared minced garlic
½ cup dried bread crumbs
¼ cup slivered almonds, crushed or ground
¼ cup coarsely chopped fresh flat-leaf parsley
1 egg, lightly beaten

TO COMPLETE THE RECIPE:

Fresh flat-leaf parsley sprigs for garnish

to make the sauce: Whisk together all the sauce ingredients in a small bowl until smooth; set aside.

to make the croquettes: Heat 1 tablespoon of the oil in a large nonstick skillet over medium-high heat. Add the yam, onion, celery, and garlic; cook, stirring occasionally, until tender, about 5 minutes. Remove from the heat and stir in all the remaining croquette ingredients.

continued »

for each patty, gently squeeze about 1 tablespoon of the mixture in your hand to form a ball, then flatten into a 2-inch round patty. Place the patties on a plate as they are prepared.

wash and dry the skillet. Add the remaining 1 tablespoon oil and heat over medium-high heat. Cook the croquettes until lightly brown and cooked through, about 3 minutes on each side. Transfer to a plate lined with paper towels; pat gently.

to serve, arrange the warm croquettes on a platter and garnish with parsley sprigs. Serve the sauce in a small bowl with a spoon or small ladle for drizzling it over the warm croquettes. Provide plates and forks for your guests.

tips Sherry is a wine to which brandy has been added to increase the flavor and alcohol content. Sherries vary in color, flavor, and sweetness. Finos are dry and light; manzanillas are very dry, delicate finos with a hint of saltiness. Olorosos, often labeled cream or golden sherry, are darker in color and sweet. Avoid using cooking sherry, which is inferior in flavor and overly salty.

What is labeled a "yam" at the supermarket in this country is really an orange sweet potato. Orange sweet potatoes have a dark, uniformly colored brown to purplish skin, a shape that tapers on both ends, and a sweet flavor when cooked. White sweet potatoes have a lighter skin, yellow flesh, and a delicately spicy, less sweet flavor. Store sweet potatoes in a cool, dark, and dry place for up to 1 week; do not refrigerate.

ADVANCE PREPARATION The sauce will keep for up to 2 days in a covered container in the refrigerator; bring to room temperature for serving. The croquette mixture will keep for up to 1 day in a covered container in the refrigerator. To serve warm, cook the croquettes just before serving or make them up to 1 day in advance, cover, and refrigerate. Reheat on a baking sheet in a preheated 350°F oven for about 5 minutes.

almond-crusted tofu cubes with sweet ginger sauce

MAKES 40 (1 CUP SAUCE)

Crispy on the outside, creamy within, these will convert even the most confirmed tofu skeptic. Allow enough time to press the tofu, making the exceptional sauce while you wait. For extra-crispy tofu, substitute panko (see Tips and Variation) for the almond coating.

12 ounces extra-firm silken tofu (see Tips)

SWEET GINGER SAUCE:

½ cup water
⅓ cup white rice vinegar (see Tips)
⅓ cup sugar
2 tablespoons soy sauce
1 tablespoon cold water
1 tablespoon cornstarch
2 teaspoons finely minced fresh ginger (see Tips)

TOFU COATING:

⅓ cup slivered almonds, crushed
⅓ cup unbleached all-purpose flour
1 tablespoon toasted wheat germ
½ teaspoon dried thyme
¼ teaspoon dried dill
¼ teaspoon sweet Hungarian paprika
¼ teaspoon freshly ground pepper
1 egg
2 tablespoons water
¼ teaspoon Tabasco sauce
1 clove garlic, minced, or ½ teaspoon prepared minced garlic
Dash of salt

TO COMPLETE THE RECIPE:

Canola oil as needed
Lettuce leaves for serving

cut the block of tofu in half horizontally, forming two ¾-inch-thick slabs. Place them on a pie plate and cover with plastic wrap. Nest another pie plate atop the plastic and place a book or other heavy object (about 3 pounds) in the plate. Let the weighted tofu stand for about 30 minutes.

meanwhile, make the sauce: Combine the water, vinegar, sugar, and soy sauce in a small saucepan. Stir constantly over medium-high heat until the mixture comes to a boil. Reduce the heat to medium-low; simmer, stirring occasionally, for about 2 minutes. Meanwhile, stir together the cold water and cornstarch in a small bowl until smooth; stir into the saucepan. Cook, stirring constantly, until the sauce is clear and slightly thickened. Remove the pan from the heat; stir in the ginger. Set aside.

to make the coating: Combine the almonds, flour, wheat germ, thyme, dill, paprika, and pepper in a small shallow bowl. Lightly beat the egg in a separate bowl; whisk in the water, Tabasco sauce, garlic, and salt.

drain off the liquid and cut the tofu into ¾-inch cubes. One at a time, gently press the tofu cubes into the flour mixture, covering all sides; dip into the egg mixture and again into the flour mixture. As the cubes are prepared, place them in a single layer on a plate.

pour oil to a depth of about ¼ inch in a large nonstick sauté pan or skillet. Heat over medium-high heat until a drop of water sizzles when added. Cook the tofu cubes in the oil, turning occasionally, until all sides are lightly browned, about 4 to 5 minutes. As they are done, use a slotted spoon or spatula to transfer the tofu to plates lined with paper towels; pat gently.

to serve, line a platter with lettuce leaves and arrange the warm tofu cubes on top; provide a container of cocktail picks. Pour the warm sauce into a small bowl for dipping. Provide plates for your guests.

continued ››

tips Panko is coarse bread crumbs used in Japanese cooking as a coating for fried foods. Look for it in Asian markets and some supermarkets.

Tofu, or bean curd, is made from soybeans. The texture varies from soft to firm depending on how much water is extracted during processing. Choose extra-firm or firm tofu if you want it to hold its sliced or cubed shape during cooking. Softer types are better for dips, sauces, and puddings, where a creamy consistency is desired.

White rice vinegar, made from fermented rice, has a low acidity and is mild and sweet. It can be found in Asian markets and most supermarkets. Look for unseasoned rice vinegar.

To preserve fresh ginger, wrap the ginger tightly in aluminum foil or seal it in a small zip-top plastic bag and freeze. When you need ginger, do not thaw; instead, simply use a fine grater to grate off the amount needed. Rewrap and replace immediately in the freezer, where the ginger will keep for up to 3 months.

VARIATION Substitute panko (see Tips) for the almond-flour coating. Follow the recipe procedure using ⅓ cup all-purpose flour for the first step in dipping the tofu cubes, then the egg mixture in the recipe, and finally ⅔ cup panko. Follow the recipe cooking procedure.

ADVANCE PREPARATION The sauce will keep for up to 3 days in a covered container in the refrigerator; bring to room temperature or reheat gently. For the best results, coat and cook the tofu just before serving.

fresh spring rolls with spicy peanut sauce

MAKES 8 PIECES (⅓ CUP SAUCE) *(vegan recipe)*

Make just one spring roll and see how easy the technique can be. For a memorable presentation, tie each spring roll half with a thin strip of scallion greens.

SPICY PEANUT SAUCE:

- 2 tablespoons creamy, unsweetened peanut butter
- 1 tablespoon Asian sesame oil
- 2 teaspoons chili paste with garlic, or to taste
- 1 teaspoon sugar
- ¼ cup water, or as needed

SPRING ROLLS:

- 1 large carrot, cut into julienne strips (see Tips)
- 4 round (8 inches in diameter) rice paper wrappers
- 2 ounces (1 small bundle) cellophane noodles (see Tips)
- ½ cucumber, halved, seeded, and cut into julienne strips
- ½ avocado, cut into thin strips
- Green parts of 2 green onions, cut into very thin 2-inch-long strips

TO COMPLETE THE RECIPE:

- Fresh cilantro or mint leaves for garnish

to make the sauce: Stir together all the sauce ingredients, except the water, in a small bowl. Stir in water as needed until the sauce is a cake-batter consistency. Taste and adjust the seasoning. Set aside.

to make the spring rolls: Steam the carrot in a covered steamer over boiling water until tender, about 4 minutes. Or, put in a microwave-proof container; add about 2 tablespoons water. Cover tightly and microwave on high for about 3 minutes. Drain well and let cool.

continued ››

while the carrot is cooking, soften the rice paper: Begin by holding a heavy-duty paper towel or thin kitchen towel under warm running water. Squeeze out the excess moisture; lay flat on the kitchen counter. Hold a sheet of rice paper under warm running water, making certain to wet both sides. Place the rice paper flat on top of the towel. Top with another layer of moist toweling, taking care to cover the edges of the rice paper. Repeat, using all of the rice paper wrappers. Let stand until the rice paper has softened, about 5 minutes. (If it stands for too long, the rice paper will become overly moist and too fragile to handle.)

meanwhile, bring a small pot of water to a boil over high heat. Add the noodles and boil for about 3 minutes, or until tender; drain well. Rinse with cool water; drain again. Using scissors, cut the noodles into shorter lengths (about 2 inches); let cool.

remove the top layer of wet toweling and discard. The filling ingredients should be arranged horizontally, leaving a 1½-inch margin of rice paper uncovered on each side. Spread about 1 teaspoon of the sauce in a horizontal line near the bottom of the paper; top with one fourth of the noodles, spreading them from side to side. Above the noodles, arrange narrow rows of the strips of carrot, cucumber, avocado, and green onion. Arrange a few cilantro or mint leaves near the top. (If the noodles begin to clump together as they cool, rinse them with cool water, loosen with your fingers, and drain.)

fold the two opposite sides of the rice paper round over the filling and to the center until the edges touch. Starting at the end closest to you, gently roll the paper and the filling, cigar style, squeezing gently as you roll. Place the completed roll, edge down, on a cutting board. Cover with a moist paper towel.

remove the next layer of toweling and repeat the procedure with the remaining rice paper rounds. (If, during the rolling process, the rice paper splits, simply moisten another round and roll it over the broken one.)

to serve, cut the spring rolls in half crosswise. Arrange them on a platter garnished with fresh cilantro or mint sprigs and accompany with a small bowl of the remaining sauce for dipping. Provide plates for your guests.

---

tips To julienne is to cut foods into matchstick strips about ⅛ inch wide.

Asian cellophane noodles, also called bean thread noodles, glass noodles, or sai fun, are made with the starch of mung beans (which we know best in the form of bean sprouts) and water. These noodles are dried and brittle, with a cellophane-like translucence. You can purchase them, coiled and wrapped in plastic, in Asian markets and in most supermarkets. They will keep indefinitely when stored in an airtight container.

VARIATIONS Try other vegetables in the filling, such as julienne strips of red bell pepper or bok choy, as well as enoki mushrooms, steamed green beans, or blanched snow peas. If you use enoki mushrooms as one of the filling ingredients, do not fold the 2 sides of the paper to the center. Instead, arrange the ingredients horizontally, all the way to the edges. Position the mushrooms so that the tiny white caps extend about an inch beyond the rice paper. Cut the spring roll into quarters, two of which will have mushrooms extending from the tops.

ADVANCE PREPARATION The Spring Rolls can be made up to 2 hours in advance. Spray them with a fine mist of water, wrap individually in plastic wrap to prevent the rice paper from drying out, and refrigerate.

layered vegetable pâtés with creamy horseradish sauce

MAKES ABOUT 12 SERVINGS (⅓ CUP SAUCE)

This recipe is simple to prepare and makes a stunning presentation. If you have a mandoline (see Tips), cut long spaghetti-like strands of carrots to line the serving plates. Drizzle the Creamy Horseradish Sauce over each slice and garnish with a sprig of fresh dill or basil.

LAYERED VEGETABLE PÂTÉS:

- 3 cups broccoli florets
- 3 cups cauliflower florets
- 3 cups thinly sliced carrots (about 6 carrots)
- 1 tablespoon olive oil
- 1 cup coarsely chopped onion
- 4 cloves garlic, minced, or 2 teaspoons prepared minced garlic
- 1 cup cooked brown rice
- 3 eggs, lightly beaten (they are used separately, so beat 1 at a time)
- ¼ cup freshly grated Parmesan cheese
- 2 tablespoons minced fresh basil, or 1 teaspoon dried basil
- 3 tablespoons fresh lemon juice, divided
- ½ teaspoon freshly ground pepper, divided
- ⅜ teaspoon salt, divided
- ¼ teaspoon red pepper flakes
- 1 tablespoon snipped fresh dill, or 1 teaspoon dried dill (see Tips)

CREAMY HORSERADISH SAUCE:

- ½ cup plain yogurt
- 2 tablespoons fresh lemon juice
- 1 tablespoon prepared horseradish sauce
- 1 tablespoon snipped fresh dill, or ½ teaspoon dried dill (see Tips)
- ¼ teaspoon Tabasco sauce, or to taste
- ⅛ teaspoon salt, or to taste

TO COMPLETE THE RECIPE:

- Fresh dill or basil sprigs for garnish

to make the pâtés: Preheat the oven to 350°F. Use vegetable-oil cooking spray to lightly oil a 5-by-9-inch loaf pan; line the bottom and long sides of the pan with waxed paper or parchment paper. Lightly spray with vegetable oil.

continued »

separately steam the broccoli, cauliflower, and carrots in a covered steamer over boiling water until tender, 5 to 6 minutes. Or, put each vegetable in a medium, microwave-proof dish; add about ¼ cup water. Cover tightly and microwave on high for about 5 minutes. Drain well. Let cool.

while the vegetables are cooking, heat the oil in a small nonstick skillet over medium heat. Add the onion and garlic; cook, stirring occasionally, until the onion is translucent, about 4 minutes. Set aside.

for the broccoli layer: Put the cooked broccoli in a food processor (or blender). Add one third of the onion mixture, ⅓ cup of the rice, 1 egg, the Parmesan, the basil, 1 tablespoon of the lemon juice, ¼ teaspoon of the pepper, and ⅛ teaspoon of the salt. Process until smooth. Spread evenly in the bottom of the prepared pan; smooth the surface.

for the cauliflower layer: Put the cooked cauliflower in a food processor (or blender). Add one third of the onion mixture, ⅓ cup of the rice, 1 egg, 1 tablespoon of the lemon juice, ⅛ teaspoon of the salt, and the red pepper flakes. Process until smooth. Spread evenly over the broccoli layer; smooth the surface.

for the carrot layer: Put the carrots in a food processor (or blender). Add the remaining onion mixture and rice, the remaining egg, and the remaining 1 tablespoon lemon juice, ¼ teaspoon pepper, and ⅛ teaspoon salt, and the dill. Process until smooth. Spread evenly over the cauliflower layer; smooth the surface. Cover with a piece of lightly oiled waxed paper.

place the loaf pan in a roasting pan and pour boiling water into the roasting pan to come about 1 inch up the sides of the loaf pan. Bake for about 1 hour and 15 minutes, or until the top of the pâtés feels firm to the touch and a knife inserted in the center comes out clean. Remove from the oven, remove the waxed paper on top, and let cool in the pan on a wire rack.

meanwhile, make the sauce: Stir together all the sauce ingredients in a small bowl. Taste and adjust the seasoning.

to serve, loosen the edges of the pâtés with a knife. Turn out of the pan onto a serving platter and peel off any waxed paper that adheres.

cut the layered pâtés into ¾-inch-thick slices. Transfer to small plates, top each serving with about 1 tablespoon of the sauce, and garnish. Provide forks for your guests.

---

tips A mandoline is a hand-operated machine with various adjustable blades for cutting firm vegetables into slices, julienne, and long, spaghetti-like strands. Mandolines can be purchased in many gourmet shops.

Dill is a sharply aromatic herb with a mild, lemony taste. When using fresh dill, cut the feathery dill tips with scissors. Dried dill is acceptable, but it is stronger than fresh, so use it in moderation.

ADVANCE PREPARATION The sauce will keep in the refrigerator for up to 2 days in a covered container. The layered pâtés can be assembled earlier on the day the dish is to be served; cover with plastic wrap and refrigerate. Bring the sauce and pâtés to room temperature for serving.

caramelized-onion frittata with chimichurri sauce

MAKES 12 SERVINGS (⅔ CUP SAUCE)

Chimichurri is an Argentinean blend of parsley, oregano, and onion puréed with olive oil, vinegar, and garlic, and cayenne. Traditionally, this vivid green sauce is an accompaniment to meat, but here it tops thin wedges of a frittata, a flat Italian omelet with the ingredients mixed into the eggs rather than folded inside, as in a French omelet.

CHIMICHURRI SAUCE:

- **2 cups loosely packed fresh flat-leaf parsley leaves**
- **¼ cup coarsely chopped onion**
- **¼ cup extra-virgin olive oil**
- **¼ cup red wine vinegar**
- **4 cloves garlic, minced, or 2 teaspoons prepared minced garlic**
- **1 teaspoon minced fresh oregano**
- **¼ teaspoon cayenne pepper, or to taste**
- **⅛ teaspoon salt, or to taste**
- **⅛ teaspoon freshly ground pepper, or to taste**

CARAMELIZED-ONION FRITTATA:

- **1 tablespoon unsalted butter**
- **1 tablespoon olive oil**
- **1 large sweet or yellow onion, halved lengthwise, each half cut lengthwise into ⅛-inch-wide strips (about 2 cups); see Tips**
- **6 eggs (see Tips)**
- **½ cup freshly grated Parmesan cheese**
- **Dash of salt and freshly ground pepper**

to make the sauce: Process all the sauce ingredients in a food processor (or blender) until smooth. Taste and adjust the seasoning. Set aside.

to make the frittata: Preheat the broiler. Melt the butter with the oil in a large, ovenproof skillet, preferably nonstick, over medium-high heat. Add the onion and cook, stirring occasionally until the onion is translucent and the water has cooked off, about 5 minutes. Reduce the heat to low; continue to cook, stirring occasionally, until the onion strips are tender and nicely browned, about 20 minutes.

continued »

while the onion is cooking, lightly beat the eggs in a medium bowl; stir in the Parmesan, salt, and pepper. When the onion is cooked, scrape up the browned bits in the bottom of the pan and pour the egg mixture into the skillet. Cook, undisturbed, until the edges and bottom of the frittata are firm, about 10 minutes.

transfer the skillet to a broiler rack. Broil 4 or 5 inches from the heating element for about 3 minutes, or just until the top of the frittata is set and lightly browned; watch closely so the eggs do not overcook.

to serve, slice the frittata into 12 thin wedges. Serve warm or at room temperature; top each serving with about 2 teaspoons of the sauce. Provide plates and forks for your guests.

tips After cooking, yellow onions usually have a sweeter flavor than white onions. Other onions particularly known for their sweetness are thinner-skinned and somewhat flatter in shape, including Vidalias from Georgia, Spring Sweets from Texas, Walla Wallas from Washington, Mauis from Hawaii, and OSO Sweets from Chile. These onions contain more sugar and water than regular onions, so they do not keep as long. They are also lower in the sulfur compounds that give most onions their characteristic bite and their power to cause tears.

Store uncooked eggs in the carton, large ends up, in the coldest part of your refrigerator (not in the refrigerator door) for up to 1 month. For the best flavor, use them within 1 week.

VARIATIONS Rather than using the broiler to finish cooking the frittata, complete it on the stovetop by lifting the cooked portions and tilting the pan to allow the uncooked parts to flow to the bottom of the pan.

Serve the frittata with Roasted Red Bell Pepper Sauce (page 22) instead of Chimichurri Sauce.

ADVANCE PREPARATION The sauce will keep for up to 2 days in a covered container in the refrigerator. Bring to room temperature to serve with a freshly made frittata.

guacamole-gouda quesadilla wedges

MAKES 8

Prepare the Guacamole and roast the bell pepper in advance, then assemble and bake the quesadilla just before serving. For a char-grilled flavor and crispier texture, toast the quesadilla in a grill pan (see Variations). The recipe for these hearty quesadillas multiplies easily, so make several at once to satisfy a hungry crowd.

Two 7-inch flour tortillas
2 tablespoons Guacamole (page 17)
¼ cup coarsely chopped Roasted Red Bell Pepper (page 21), or jarred roasted red bell pepper, well drained
Dash of salt and freshly ground pepper
¼ cup coarsely shredded Gouda or smoked Gouda cheese (see Tip)

preheat the oven to 375°F. Place 1 tortilla on a baking sheet. Spread with the Guacamole, leaving a 1-inch border. Arrange the bell pepper atop the Guacamole; sprinkle with salt and pepper. Add a layer of cheese. Top with the other tortilla, pressing down gently to make the filling adhere.

bake for about 8 minutes, or until the cheese is melted and the tortillas are softened and warm.

to serve: Cut the quesadilla into 8 wedges. Serve warm. Provide plates for your guests.

---

tip Gouda cheese, which is imported from Holland and also made in the United States, has a mild, nutlike flavor. It can be made from whole or part-skim cow's milk and is aged from a few weeks to over a year. The cheese comes in large wheels with a yellow wax rind; baby Gouda, available in most supermarkets, has a red wax coating.

VARIATIONS Substitute pepper Jack or Monterey Jack cheese for the Gouda.

Rather than baking the assembled quesadilla, toast it on a dry stovetop grill pan. Heat the pan over medium-high heat, then toast the quesadilla until the cheese is melted and grill marks are visible on the tortillas, 4 to 6 minutes per side.

apple and caramelized-onion pizza triangles

MAKES 16

Pita bread makes a fine, thin, and simple crust, perfect for this rich onion, cheese, and walnut topping. The onion mixture can be caramelized ahead of time, but you should assemble and broil the pizzas just before serving.

- 2 tablespoons olive oil, plus more for brushing
- 1 large sweet or yellow onion, halved vertically and each half cut lengthwise into ⅛-inch-wide strips (see Tips, page 43)
- 1 cup diced tart apple, such as Granny Smith or Haralson
- 2 tablespoons balsamic vinegar
- 2 teaspoons sugar
- Salt and freshly ground pepper to taste
- One 6- or 7-inch pita bread round, split horizontally
- 1 cup (4 ounces) coarsely shredded mozzarella cheese (see Tip)
- ¼ cup coarsely chopped toasted walnuts (see Tip, page 58)

heat the 2 tablespoons oil in a large nonstick skillet over medium-high heat; add the onion and cook, stirring occasionally, for about 5 minutes, or until translucent. Reduce the heat to low; add the apple, vinegar, and sugar. Continue to cook, stirring occasionally, until the onion strips are very tender and nicely browned, about 15 minutes. Add salt and pepper to taste. Remove from the heat and set aside.

preheat the broiler. Place the pita halves, rough-side up, on a baking sheet. Lightly brush with oil. Broil 4 to 5 inches from the heat source for about 1 minute, or until lightly toasted.

to assemble the pizzas, spread the crusts with the cheese and top with the onion mixture. Sprinkle with the walnuts. Broil for 1½ to 2 minutes, or until the cheese is melted.

to serve, cut each pizza into 8 wedges and serve immediately. Provide plates for your guests.

---

tip Firm, semifirm, and semisoft cheeses should be wrapped airtight in a plastic bag; store in the refrigerator cheese compartment or in the warmest part of the refrigerator for up to several weeks. Mold can be cut away if it develops.

VARIATIONS Substitute a pear, such as red or green Bartlett or Bosc, for the apple.

Sprinkle the pizzas with about 2 tablespoons minced, well-drained, oil-packed sun-dried tomatoes before broiling.

ADVANCE PREPARATION The onion mixture can be cooked up to 1 day in advance; cover and refrigerate. Bring to room temperature before assembling the pizzas.

tortilla pinwheels

MAKES 16 (½ CUP CHIPOTLE SPREAD)

Make multicolored pinwheels with sun-dried tomato or spinach tortillas. The chipotle spread packs quite a kick, so beware! To tone it down, add less chipotle chile or substitute minced jalapeños. For an attractive presentation, purée ¼ cup chopped mango with 2 tablespoons fresh orange juice. Pour the sweet sauce into a plastic squeeze bottle and draw lines on the serving plate, top with the pinwheels, and sprinkle the plate with finely diced red bell pepper.

CHIPOTLE SPREAD:

½ cup cream cheese at room temperature
1 tablespoon fresh orange juice
1 tablespoon minced fresh chives or green onion (green part only)
2 teaspoons minced, soaked, and drained chipotle chile, or to taste (see Tip)

TORTILLA ROLLS:

Two 10-inch flour tortillas
¼ cup fresh cilantro leaves
½ Roasted Red Bell Pepper (page 21), or ½ jarred roasted red bell pepper, well drained, cut lengthwise into ¼-inch-wide strips
½ mango, cut lengthwise into ¼-inch-wide strips

to make the chipotle spread: Stir together all the spread ingredients in a small bowl until smooth. Taste and adjust the seasoning.

to assemble the tortilla rolls: Spread 1 tortilla with half of the chipotle spread. Sprinkle with half of the cilantro leaves. Starting about 1 inch up from the bottom of the tortilla, arrange 1 row of the bell pepper strips and another of the mango strips, keeping the ingredients in the bottom third of the tortilla. Fold the bottom of the tortilla over the filling, then firmly roll away from you. Repeat with the second tortilla. Wrap the rolls in plastic wrap and refrigerate for at least 15 minutes.

unwrap the rolls and trim to even the ends. Using a serrated knife in a sawing motion, cut each roll into eight 1-inch-thick slices.

to serve: Arrange the slices, cut side down, on a platter. Provide plates for your guests.

continued »

tip Chipotle chilies are dried and smoked jalapeños. They have a dark brown, wrinkled skin and a very hot, smoky flavor. Purchase them dried in specialty markets and some supermarkets. To soften before using, pour boiling water over the chilies in a small bowl and soak for about 30 to 45 minutes, depending on the size of the chilies.

VARIATION For larger servings, cut the rolls into thicker diagonal slices.

ADVANCE PREPARATION The spread will keep for up to 2 days in a covered container in the refrigerator. The plastic-wrapped rolls can be refrigerated for up to 4 hours before serving; slice into pinwheels just before serving.

SWEET BITES

Add a sweet note by serving these after savory, salty, and cheesy appetizers. You may offer them in an area of the buffet table throughout the evening, but bringing them out later in the event is an unexpected surprise and also signals that the party's almost over.

These sweet bites complement the other appetizers in this book. Whimsical Hazelnut-Meringue Mushrooms (page 130) and intriguing Chèvre-Cherry Bonbons (page 133) are light and not overly sweet. If you're a chocolate fan—and who isn't—dip some large long-stemmed strawberries into dark chocolate for a juicy, sweet treat that will add style to the setting.

hazelnut-meringue mushrooms

MAKES ABOUT 36

These sweet, airy mushrooms add whimsy to an appetizer buffet. Make them well in advance, because they will keep for up to 2 weeks at room temperature in an airtight container. If you haven't worked with meringue before, begin by reading the Tips to guarantee your success.

- ¾ cup powdered sugar
- ¼ cup (1 ounce) toasted unskinned hazelnuts, finely ground (see Tip, page 58)
- 2 tablespoons cornstarch
- 4 egg whites (see Tips)
- ⅔ cup granulated sugar
- ¼ teaspoon unsweetened cocoa powder
- 2 ounces semisweet chocolate, chopped

preheat the oven to 200°F. Line 2 baking sheets with parchment paper.

stir together the powdered sugar, hazelnuts, and cornstarch in a small bowl; set aside.

in a large bowl, beat the egg whites until foamy. Gradually beat in the granulated sugar until stiff, glossy peaks form. Using a rubber spatula, fold in the powdered sugar mixture (see Tips).

transfer the meringue to a large pastry bag fitted with a ½-inch plain tip. To make the mushroom stems, pipe 18 dome shapes about ¾ inch wide at the bottom and 1 inch tall, tapering to a point at the top. To make the mushroom caps, pipe 18 round half-sphere shapes (about 1½ inches wide at the bottom and ¾ to 1 inch tall) onto the baking sheets. Use your fingers to smooth the tops of the caps, if necessary. Dust the stems and caps lightly with cocoa powder stirred through a very fine-meshed sieve.

bake for about 2 hours, or until crisp and completely dry. Let cool on the baking sheets on a wire rack. Gently remove the cookies from the paper.

melt the chocolate in a double boiler over barely simmering water (see Tip, page 134), stirring occasionally until smooth.

continued »

remove the pan from the heat. Using a small spoon, place a ¾-inch-wide dollop of chocolate on the flat side of a mushroom cap. Use a sharp knife to trim the pointed tip from a mushroom stem so that it is flat. Attach a stem to the cap while the chocolate is soft; press gently. Place the mushroom, stem up, on a plate. Repeat to form the remaining mushrooms. Refrigerate, uncovered, until the chocolate is set, about 20 minutes.

tips To separate egg whites from yolks, separate 1 egg at a time into a cup or small bowl. The most basic method is with your hand. Cup your hand and crack the egg into it; the white slips through your fingers while the yolk stays in your palm. Or, use an egg separator or funnel. It's not a good idea to separate eggs by passing the yolk back and forth from one half of a shell to the other because minute bacteria on the shell's surface might be transfered to the egg.

Transfer each white to the mixing bowl only after it is successfully separated, as even a tiny drop of yolk can hinder foam formation. It is also important that the bowl and beaters are spotlessly clean and free from any oil. It's best to use glass or stainless-steel bowls, since plastic may retain a film of oil. Eggs separate more easily when they are refrigerator-cold, but the whites will whip to greater volume if they stand at room temperature for about 20 minutes before beating.

Gentle folding is the key to maintaining volume when adding ingredients to stiff egg whites. Use a rubber spatula, combining the mixtures with a downward stroke into the bowl, continuing across the bottom, up the side, and over the top of the mixture. Come up through the center every few strokes and rotate the bowl frequently as you fold. Fold just until the ingredients are combined.

VARIATION For quicker preparation, use the meringue to make drop cookies. Simply drop the batter by tablespoons onto the baking sheets, lined with parchment paper.

ADVANCE PREPARATION Store the completed mushrooms for up to 1 week in an airtight container at room temperature.

chèvre-cherry bonbons

MAKES 12

An unusual contrast of tart cheese, dark cherries, and semisweet chocolate, these tidbits are a lovely surprise. They're simple to make in advance, and I guarantee they will impress even your most discriminating guests.

5 ounces chilled fresh, white goat cheese
1 tablespoon powdered sugar
6 canned dark pitted cherries in heavy syrup, drained
4 ounces semisweet chocolate, coarsely chopped

mix the cheese and sugar in a medium bowl until well blended. (The mixture will look crumbly.)

to make the filling: Spread the cherries on a paper towel and gently pat dry. Spoon about ½ tablespoon of the cheese mixture into your hand and gently press to flatten. Place a cherry half in the center, then gently roll between your hands to form a ball as you cover the cherry with cheese. Repeat with the remaining cheese and cherries.

arrange the balls in a single layer on 2 small plates and cover with plastic wrap. Freeze for about 1 hour. Meanwhile, line a baking sheet with aluminum foil or parchment paper.

to make the bonbons: Melt the chocolate in a double boiler over barely simmering water (see Tip), stirring occasionally until smooth. Remove the pan from the heat.

remove one plate of cheese balls from the freezer. Using a candy-dipping tool or a spoon, immerse one ball in the melted chocolate; gently roll to coat it. Lift and tilt the dipping utensil to allow the excess chocolate to drain back into the pan. Place the bonbon on the prepared baking sheet. Dip the remaining cheese balls. (Work quickly, because it is important that the cheese balls remain frozen during this step.)

continued ››

refrigerate the bonbons until the chocolate is set, about 5 minutes. Transfer the bonbons in a single layer to an airtight refrigerator container for storage. Serve chilled.

tip When using a double boiler, adjust the level of the simmering water so it does not touch the bottom of the upper pan. This allows for gentle heating of sensitive foods such as chocolate, custards, and delicate sauces.

VARIATION Substitute dates for the cherries. Depending on the size of the dates, use halves or thirds for each bonbon. Press them into a ball before covering them with the cheese. (If the entire recipe is made with dates, it will yield about 16 bonbons.)

ADVANCE PREPARATION If the bonbons are made with very fresh cheese, they will keep for up to 5 days in a tightly closed container in the refrigerator. Or, freeze them for up to 2 weeks; thaw in the refrigerator.

candied brie with apple wedges

MAKES 4 SERVINGS

This recipe makes candied apples for grown-ups as elegant as they are finger-licking good. For a larger group, buy a larger round of Brie and multiply the sauce ingredients. Serve plain Wonton Wedges (page 25) on the side for an interesting presentation and added crunch.

One 4-inch round Brie cheese
1 tablespoon unsalted butter
2 tablespoons firmly packed light brown sugar
Juice of ½ lemon
1 large tart apple, such as Granny Smith, cut into about 12 wedges
5 pecan halves

preheat the oven to 275°F. Place the Brie on a baking sheet. Bake for about 15 minutes, or until softened and warm.

meanwhile, melt the butter in a small nonstick saucepan over medium heat. Reduce the heat to medium-low; add the brown sugar and stir occasionally until melted.

make acidulated water by mixing the lemon juice into a small bowl of water. Dip the apple wedges in the water (see Tip).

place the warm cheese in a small serving bowl or on a small plate. Drizzle with the warm sauce. Garnish with the pecans in a pinwheel formation. Surround the cheese with the apple wedges.

provide plates for your guests and small knives for spreading the cheese on the apples.

---

tip Acidulated water is water to which a small amount of an acid, such as lemon, lime, or orange juice, has been added. Dipping fruits, such as apples and pears, in this liquid prevents their cut surfaces from darkening when they are exposed to air.

VARIATION Substitute a pear for the apple.

chocolate-glazed strawberries

MAKES 16

Brilliant strawberries cloaked in glossy, dark chocolate make an impressive dessert or garnish. Use large berries with long elegant stems. I like to arrange them on a platter with Chèvre-Cherry Bonbons (page 133) or use them to add color to other appetizer platters. The same chocolate-glazing technique can be used for other fresh fruits, such as pineapple slices and orange segments, or for dried fruit or nuts.

16 large fresh strawberries, hulls and stems attached

6 ounces semisweet chocolate, coarsely chopped (see Tip)

Fresh mint sprigs for garnish

wash the berries and dry thoroughly. Line a baking sheet with waxed paper or parchment paper.

melt the chocolate in a double boiler over barely simmering water (see Tip, page 134), stirring occasionally until smooth. Remove the pan from the heat.

using a small rubber spatula or spoon and working over the pan, spread a berry about halfway up the side with chocolate. Place on the prepared baking sheet. Repeat to glaze all the remaining berries. Refrigerate until the chocolate is set, about 10 minutes. Transfer the berries, in a single layer, to a covered container and refrigerate until serving.

to serve, arrange the chilled strawberries on a plate garnished with mint.

---

tip Chocolate should be stored, tightly wrapped, in a cool, dry place, where it will keep for years. Because it scorches easily, it should be melted in a double boiler over barely simmering water (see Tip, page 134), or in a microwave on medium.

ADVANCE PREPARATION The strawberries can be spread with chocolate early the day they are to be served; cover and refrigerate.

fruit kabobs

MAKES 16

Vary the fruit, if you like, but definitely use avocado, a fruit usually thought of as a vegetable. Its creamy texture and mild, nutty flavor are a luscious surprise. If time permits, cut the pineapple into triangles, the avocado into cubes, and the banana into rounded chunks, leaving the tangerine sections and strawberries whole. (Any odd pieces of fruit that remain can be blended with yogurt and orange juice as a treat for the cook.)

BASTING SAUCE:

2 tablespoons melted butter
2 tablespoons fresh lemon juice
2 tablespoons honey
¼ teaspoon ground allspice

TO COMPLETE THE RECIPE:

2 tangerines, peeled and cut into 1-inch cubes
2 large bananas, peeled and cut into 1-inch-thick slices
1 avocado, peeled, pitted, and cut into 1-inch cubes
Sixteen 1-inch cubes fresh pineapple (about ¼ pineapple)
16 fresh strawberries, hulled

soak sixteen 6-inch wooden skewers in water for 30 minutes; drain. Meanwhile, preheat the broiler. Line a baking sheet with aluminum foil.

to make the basting sauce: Stir together all the sauce ingredients in a small bowl.

thread the fruit onto the skewers in the order listed. Lightly brush the sauce on all sides of the fruit.

broil the skewers 4 to 5 inches from the heating element for about 3 minutes, or until the fruit is just heated through but not cooked. Serve warm or at room temperature. Provide plates and forks for your guests.

dessert canapés

MAKES 16 (½ CUP RICOTTA MIXTURE)

A mixture of sweetened ricotta, chocolate, fruit, and nuts is a versatile topping or a dip for cookies, or try it as a quick-to-prepare filling for edible dessert containers.

RICOTTA MIXTURE:

- ½ cup (4 ounces) whole milk ricotta cheese
- 1 teaspoon coarsely chopped orange zest (see Tip)
- 1 tablespoon fresh orange juice
- 1 teaspoon honey, or to taste
- ⅛ teaspoon pure almond extract
- 2 tablespoons slivered almonds, coarsely chopped
- 2 tablespoons semisweet chocolate chips
- 1 tablespoon dried currants

TO COMPLETE THE RECIPE:

- 16 gingersnaps or thin chocolate wafers
- Sweetened cocoa powder for garnish
- 16 fresh raspberries

to make the ricotta mixture: Stir together the ricotta cheese, orange zest, orange juice, honey, and almond extract in a medium bowl until smooth. Stir in the almonds, chocolate chips, and currants.

spoon a ½-tablespoon dollop of the ricotta mixture in the center of each gingersnap or chocolate wafer. Dust with cocoa powder stirred through a very fine-meshed sieve. Top with a raspberry.

---

tip To remove citrus zest, use a zester, which has a short, flat blade with a beveled end and 5 small holes. When drawn firmly over the skin of a citrus fruit, the tool removes thin strips of the colored zest. (Do not strip off the white pith beneath; it has a bitter flavor.) Or, use a vegetable peeler to remove strips of the zest, then use a knife to thinly slice or mince the strips.

VARIATIONS Spoon the ricotta mixture into mini filo-dough shells, available in the freezer section of most supermarkets.

Stuff the ricotta mixture into mini cannoli shells, which can be purchased in Italian delis and some supermarkets.

ADVANCE PREPARATION The ricotta mixture will keep for up to 3 days in a covered container in the refrigerator. Assemble the canapés up to 1 hour before serving.

appendix: vegan recipes

The following recipes fit into the vegan designation:

APPETIZER BASICS

- Basil Pesto
- Red Pepper–Corn Salsa
- Roasted Garlic
- Roasted Red Bell Peppers
- Roasted Red Bell Pepper Sauce
- Crostini *
- Bagel Chips *
- Crispy Tortilla Triangles *
- Croustades *
- Toast Points *
- Toasted Tortilla Cups *

LIGHT BITES

- Spicy Black Bean Spread
- Roasted Red Pepper Hummus
- Moroccan Carrot Spread with Pita *
- Chutney–Hot Chile Tortilla Canapes *
- Mango-Pomegranate Salsa with Crispy Tortilla Triangles *
- Pesto Palmiers

MEZZO BITES

- Crunchy Szechuan Green Beans
- Greek Green Beans and Tomatoes
- Mixed Mushroom–Almond Pâté

SIZABLE BITES

- Five-Spice Diced Vegetables in Endive Leaves with Plum Sauce
- Herbed Diced Vegetables in Crisp New Potato Cups
- Fresh Spring Rolls with Spicy Peanut Sauce

* *Check ingredients labels of bread, tortilla, or pita.*

index

table of equivalents

The exact equivalents in the following tables have been rounded for convenience.

LIQUID AND DRY MEASURES

U.S.	METRIC
¼ teaspoon	1.25 milliliters
½ teaspoon	2.5 milliliters
1 teaspoon	5 milliliters
1 tablespoon (3 teaspoons)	15 milliliters
1 fluid ounce (2 tablespoons)	30 milliliters
¼ cup	60 milliliters
⅓ cup	80 milliliters
1 cup	240 milliliters
1 pint (2 cups)	480 milliliters
1 quart (4 cups, 32 ounces)	960 milliliters
1 gallon (4 quarts)	3.84 liters
1 ounce (by weight)	28 grams
1 pound	454 grams
2.2 pounds	1 kilogram

LENGTH MEASURES

U.S.	METRIC
⅛ inch	3 millimeters
¼ inch	6 millimeters
½ inch	12 millimeters
1 inch	2.5 centimeters

OVEN TEMPERATURES

FAHRENHEIT	CELSIUS	GAS
250	120	½
275	140	1
300	150	2
325	160	3
350	180	4
375	190	5
400	200	6
425	220	7
450	230	8
475	240	9
500	260	10